TRENT C. BUTLER

*A Lesson Commentary for Use with the
International Sunday School Lessons*

Points

for Emphasis

1995-1996

BROADMAN
& HOLMAN
PUBLISHERS

Nashville, Tennessee

Table of Contents

■ **FIRST QUARTER:**
The Story of Christian Beginnings
(The Acts)

■ **SECOND QUARTER:**
God's Promise of Deliverance

UNIT II: THE MINISTRY OF THE SUFFERING SERVANT

GOD'S LOVE FOR ALL PEOPLE

■ THIRD QUARTER:
Teachings of Jesus

UNIT I: TEACHINGS ABOUT THE KINGDOM OF HEAVEN

UNIT II: TEACHING ABOUT GOD

UNIT III: TEACHINGS ABOUT LIVING

■ FOURTH QUARTER:
A Practical Religion (James)

■ God Is With Us (Psalms)

UNIT I: PRAISING GOD

UNIT II: RESPONDING TO GOD

■ Alternative lesson for January 21st

Good News!

That's the church in a nutshell. Or maybe it is Jesus in a sound byte but not the church.

This year is inventory time for you and your church. As you study Acts, Isaiah, Jonah, Ruth, James, Psalms, and the Gospels, one theme keeps ringing through. God wants good news. Somehow, we react like Jonah. We hear only bad news. So . . .

we flee God.

we say as little as possible about God.

we pray only in emergencies and then for our needs.

we complain bitterly about God's mission and person.

we prefer death to life like it is.

Or . . .are you like Ruth:

steadfast and true, even among foreigners.

willing to work, whatever the mission God gives.

glad to obey older, wiser voices.

desiring to do your part, no matter how humble.

open for God's use and surprised at how He works.

What makes the difference. Acts has an answer: the Spirit gives you power for mission.

The Gospels have an answer: Jesus has brought the kingdom, made you part of it, and shown you what life in the kingdom is like.

Isaiah contributes good news: bad times can be forgotten. God has a plan for you, as His servant.

James sums it all up: faith puts you to work ignoring people's differences, concentrating on life in the kingdom Jesus described and brought.

What does all this have to do with inventory time? It means you as an individual, your class, and your church need to take stock. Are you Jonah? or Ruth? Purveyors of good news? or bad? Working in the kingdom? or against it? Bringing guilt? or forgiveness? Keep score this year. Will good news win out over bad in your life? in your teaching? in the life of your church?

I have promised the Bible class I teach one thing: every lesson will end with good news. Does your class need good news more than anything else? Together, let us help them find that good news this year. The news is good only as the Spirit, the kingdom, servanthood, and faith combine to produce good news in the life you and I live each day.

Books from BROADMAN & HOLMAN
for Studying and Teaching

Layman's Bible Book Commentary,
    Volumes 4,8,10,13,15,17,18,19,23.
The Broadman Bible Commentary,
    Volumes 2,4,5,7,8,9,10,11
The New American Commentary,
    Volumes 19b, 22,24,26
Atlas of the Bible Lands,
    Harry Thomas Frank, ed.
Old Testament Survey,
    Paul R. House
Introducing the New Testament,
    Joe Blair
Learning to Study the Bible,
    Earl P. McQuay
Holman Bible Dictionary,
    Trent C. Butler, ed.
Holman Bible Handbook,
    David Dockery, ed.
Holman Book of Charts, Maps, and Reconstructions,
    Marsha Ellis Smith, ed.
Pronouncing Bible Names, Expanded Edition,
    W. Murray Severance
The Prophets as Preachers,
    Gary V. Smith
The Person and Work of the Holy Spirit,
    Donald T. Williams

The Promise of the Spirit's Power

ACTS 1:1-14

Paris lay out before me, startling me with its quaint beauty. More startling, this young man from West Texas was going to live in this storied atmosphere of Europe. How did all that come about? A year earlier I would never have suspected this. Never did I think I would move from the jobless market to the European market. In His mighty way, God opened the door to mission. I walked through with Him. I could relate to those early Christians gathered in Jerusalem wondering what would happen next. You and I will watch what happened as we study the Book of Acts for the next thirteen weeks. We will see how God does missions, how His Holy Spirit empowers ordinary people, and how insurmountable barriers fall before His plans.

■ THE BIBLE LESSON

1 The former treatise have I made, O Theophilus, of all that Jesus began both to do and teach,

2 Until the day in which he was taken up, after that he through the Holy Ghost had given commandments unto the apostles whom he had chosen:

3 To whom also he showed himself alive after his passion by many infallible proofs, being seen of them forty days, and speaking of the things pertaining to the kingdom of God:

4 And, being assembled together with them, commanded them that they should not depart from Jerusalem, but wait for the promise of the Father, which, saith he, ye have heard of me.

5 For John truly baptized with water; but ye shall be baptized with the Holy Ghost not many days hence.

6 When they therefore were come together, they asked of him, saying, Lord, wilt thou at this time restore again the kingdom to Israel?

7 And he said unto them, It is not for you to know the times or the sea-

sons, which the Father hath put in his own power.

8 But ye shall receive power, after that the Holy Ghost is come upon you: and ye shall be witnesses unto me both in Jerusalem, and in all Judea, and in Samaria, and unto the uttermost part of the earth.

9 And when he had spoken these things, while they beheld, he was taken up; and a cloud received him out of their sight.

10 And while they looked steadfastly toward heaven as he went up, behold, two men stood by them in white apparel;

11 Which also said, Ye men of Galilee, why stand ye gazing up into heaven? this same Jesus, which is taken up from you into heaven, shall so come in like manner as ye have seen him go into heaven.

12 Then returned they unto Jerusalem from the mount called Olivet, which is from Jerusalem a sabbath day's journey.

13 And when they were come in, they went up into an upper room, where abode both Peter, and James, and John, and Andrew, Philip, and Thomas, Bartholomew, and Matthew, James the son of Alphaeus, and Simon Zelotes, and Judas the brother of James.

14 These all continued with one accord in prayer and supplication, with the women, and Mary the mother of Jesus, and with his brethren.

■ THE LESSON EXPLAINED

The Powerful Prologue (vv. 1–2)

Continued next week. What a frustrating note to see at the bottom of the screen. We are not the first to see it. Luke, the Bible's most famous doctor (Col. 4:14), made his friend Theophilus wait for the second volume of the Jesus story. For Luke, the story did not end where his Gospel ended. The story ended only when the known world had heard the gospel message. Volume 2 had to come. His Gentile friend, whose name meant "lover of God," needed to know how the gospel spread from a bunch of scared Jews to Rome, the center of universal politics and civilization.

The how could be summarized in one phrase: the Holy Spirit. In his Gospel Luke had pictured the Spirit with Jesus and only with Jesus (3:22; 4:1,14,18). Now the Spirit would rest on the apostles. The Spirit tied Gospel and Acts together. The Spirit would take the teachings of Jesus and spread them around the world.

The Power Promise (vv. 3–8)

Eleven men, a few women, and some anonymous hangers-on stayed together after Jesus' ascension. Why? What hope did they have? The Jews accused them of body-snatching. The Romans had crucified their leader for treason and might well do the same to them. Two things kept them together. They had seen the resurrected Christ, and they had a promise of power. What kind of power? They were not really sure. Political dreams still lingered (v. 6), but He did not exactly encourage them. Rather, He commanded, wait until you have the Spirit's power. Then you will witness for Me. Witness of what? Witness to the uttermost parts of the world. How could this small, uneducated, untraveled group do that? Why was He so secretive? Could He not reveal something to give them hope? If not, the promise of Holy Spirit power sufficed. They would wait.

Prayer Power (vv. 9–14)

How do you occupy time waiting? Certainly, they rehearsed together all their experiences with Jesus. In a sense, all the Gospels began to be written there in the upper room as the apostles bided their time reminiscing. They not only told the Jesus stories, they raised their questions with one another. What is next? The angels said He would come back. He said He would send the Holy Spirit. He would not tell us the times. What are we waiting for?

One way to find out. Ask Him. Jesus had taught the disciples to pray. Now they put that teaching into practice. Together they asked God to answer their questions. They asked for patience to wait. They asked what He wanted them to do. Gradually, they found the power of prayer, for some answers began to come. Peter learned that they needed to replace Judas (vv. 15–26). How? Through prayer and through reading Scripture (v. 16). So as answers began to come, faith grew, patience remained, and so did the promise.

■ TRUTHS TO LIVE BY

Faith rests on resurrection. Scared to death, the apostles fled the cross in all directions. Only John and the women watched the crucifixion. Even the first resurrection experience left them frightened speechless (Mark 16:8). As they gathered together, sharing resurrection experiences and talking with the resurrected Lord drew them back into a team ready to wait together for the Lord's next move. So, too, we are foolish if we serve Christ without firm resurrection hope. The resurrection makes our faith different from all others.

Faith rests on promise. Jesus had the Spirit. The disciples had to wait for it. They waited because they had Jesus' promise. If they had not waited, Pentecost would have never happened. We, too, wait: to know our personal mission, to receive His power, to see the church accept the mission we have individually, to see people we witness to respond, to experience the church revival and national awakening for which we pray, to see loved ones healed. Waiting is a large part of faith. We wait because He promised.

Faith lives on prayer. Waiting is not enough. Life with God is an experience of a love relationship. We wait with faith because we converse with Him daily. He hears us. We hear Him. We see what He is doing in our world. We find how we can be part of what He is doing. We listen to Him speak through the Bible. We believe in the resurrection. We trust His promises. We live daily by talking with Him in prayer. That is the Christian life.

■ A VERSE TO REMEMBER

Ye shall receive power, after that the Holy Ghost is come upon you: and ye shall be witnesses unto me both in Jerusalem, and in all Judea, and in Samaria, and unto the uttermost part of the earth.—Acts 1:8

■ DAILY BIBLE READINGS

Aug. 28 — The Spirit's Prediction. Acts 1:15–20
Aug. 29 — God Works Through the Spirit. Zech. 4:1–6
Aug. 30 — Empowered by the Spirit. Matt. 12:22–28
Aug. 31 — The Holy Spirit's Work. John 16:1–15
Sept. 1 — Life in the Spirit. Rom. 8:11–17,26–27
Sept. 2 — The Spirit Gives Life. 2 Cor. 3:1–6
Sept. 3 — God's Affirmation. 1 John 4:13–18

The Holy Spirit's Coming in Power

ACTS 2:1-4,14A,29-33,37-39,44-45

Doubts flooded my life. Changes at work seemed to question my abilities and alter my calling. Other normal life experiences increased the confusion. Friends and colleagues crowded conflicting advice into my whirling brain. Stop! Halt! Enough human words. I stepped back with my wife and started seeking God's will. Nothing extraordinary resulted . . . at least nothing you can describe in Damascus Road terms. Three different people came to me with a product idea—the same one, one I had been contemplating myself. Opportunity came for me to visit a summer conference center where Henry Blackaby was explaining his *Experiencing God* understanding of life. Suddenly, everything clicked. Confidence flooded back. The *Experiencing God Bible* constituted my calling for the next year. Words started rolling off the format. A relatively new employee devised a page format. The new work organization gave me assistance on technical parts of the project. Less than a month later as I am writing these *Points*, the New Testament materials are complete. Why? Because I suddenly dedicated myself to work and showed how brilliant I could be? Hardly!

One explanation alone satisfies me. God had a new work to do. He sent the Holy Spirit to get me started. When I finally quit listening to people and opened my life to the Spirit, creative work began. The Spirit still lives. He still works through ordinary people. Even you!

■ THE BIBLE LESSON

1 *And when the day of Pentecost was fully come, they were all with one accord in one place.*

2 *And suddenly there came a sound from heaven as of a rushing mighty wind, and it filled all the house where they were sitting.*

3 *And there appeared unto them cloven tongues like as of fire, and it*

sat upon each of them.

4 And they were all filled with the Holy Ghost, and began to speak with other tongues, as the Spirit gave them utterance.

. . . .

14 But Peter, standing up with the eleven, lifted up his voice, and said unto them, . . .

. . . .

29 Men and brethren, let me freely speak unto you of the patriarch David, that he is both dead and buried, and his sepulchre is with us unto this day.

30 Therefore being a prophet, and knowing that God had sworn with an oath to him, that of the fruit of his loins, according to the flesh, he would raise up Christ to sit on his throne;

31 He seeing this before spake of the resurrection of Christ, that his soul was not left in hell, neither his flesh did see corruption.

32 This Jesus hath God raised up, whereof we all are witnesses.

33 Therefore being by the right hand of God exalted, and having received of the Father the promise of the Holy Ghost, he hath shed forth this, which ye now see and hear.

. . . .

37 Now when they heard this, they were pricked in their heart, and said unto Peter and to the rest of the apostles, Men and brethren, what shall we do?

38 Then Peter said unto them, Repent, and be baptized every one of you in the name of Jesus Christ for the remission of sins, and ye shall receive the gift of the Holy Ghost.

39 For the promise is unto you, and to your children, and to all that are afar off, even as many as the Lord our God shall call.

. . . .

44 And all that believed were together, and had all things common;

45 And sold their possessions and goods, and parted them to all men, as every man had need.

■ THE LESSON EXPLAINED

Power to Witness (2:1–13)

No other day like it. In all history this day stands alone. Weak, wondering, working people gained power that changed the life of everyone who has since lived on earth. What kind of power is this? How did it come? Can I have it?

In total agreement 120 people looked for the same thing, refusing to argue, helping one another, staying together in the same room. Then came the power. A wind blew in. They heard it. Fire flashed on their heads. They saw it. The Holy Spirit took up residence in each of them. They felt Him. They could speak languages they never knew before. People from all over the world understood them. Total confusion. Why? Because the crowd had total clarity. No one needed an interpreter. Each understood the message about Jesus. Where did such clarity come from? These uneducated men and women could not speak like this yesterday.

Oh, that's not power. They're just drunk. Wait a bit. Everything will calm down.

Power to Preach (2:14–36)

That's not right. We are not drunk.

Peter took charge. We have not even had time to get drunk. It's nine o'clock in the morning. Prayer time. No one has eaten yet, much less begun to drink. Let me give you the real explanation! You have Jewish backgrounds. You know Scripture. The prophet Joel (2:28–32) prepared you for this. God's Spirit has come. He has given us all power to preach about Jesus. He is inviting you to call on Jesus' name and be saved. Only then will you be God's people.

What do you mean, Peter? Jesus is dead. We saw Him die on the cross. What nonsense are you saying?

Yes, Jesus died. You killed Him. But only because God had planned it that way. God gave Jesus to die so you could have the Spirit's power to live. Death was not the end. God had planned that, too. He raised Jesus from the grave. Psalm 16:8–11 and 110:1 should have prepared you for that. Jesus ascended to heaven and sent His Spirit down to us. This means one thing. Jesus is the Master, the Lord. You must obey Him. Jesus is the Messiah. He is your only source of hope.

Power to Change (2:37–47)

The evidence is clear. No power like this ever appeared on

earth. Peter, what should we do? What can we do? Tell us!

Simple. Change your life. Turn away from self, from sin, from religion for religion's sake. Turn to Christ. Obey Him.

How do we obey?

First, be baptized. This shows the world that you have repented, that you are dead to all old ways of life. You have become a new person in Jesus. He has washed away your sins. They are forgiven and remembered no more. Guilt is gone. You are free to serve Christ.

Three thousand heard the powerful witnessing and powerful preaching. Three thousand were baptized. Three thousand more received the powerful Spirit. And unity prevailed among 3,120. They helped each other. No need went unmet. That is power!

■ TRUTHS TO LIVE BY

Power is available. Life need not remain powerless, dreary, routine. The Holy Spirit still comes to live in His people. He shows where God is working, gives you a task to do, and gives you power to complete the task.

Power changes lives. Repentance precedes power. You must want your life changed. You must turn away from every source of power you know. You must turn to God for power. Then He changes your life. In doing so, He names the direction of change, not you.

Power creates the church. The Holy Spirit does not feature super heroes. He blends people into the church of Jesus Christ. He gives each power that the church needs to meet needs within and without the church. The Spirit does not create competition to see who totals the best score. The Spirit creates cooperation to show the world a powerful body at work together in ways the world has never seen.

■ A VERSE TO REMEMBER

Repent, and be baptized every one of you in the name of Jesus Christ for the remission of sins, and ye shall receive the gift of the Holy Ghost.—Acts 2:38

■ DAILY BIBLE READINGS

Healing and Preaching
ACTS 3:1-8; 4:5-12

Andy introduced me to the world of the physically challenged. He came to church whenever the doors opened. We knew little about ramps and easy access back then. Only great creativity and some strong football players got Andy through the church labyrinths to our youth meeting halls. Somehow, Andy always got there with the biggest smile of all. Andy was also the first of my friends to leave this world and enter the next. We never understood why so many prayers for such a courageous and loving child did not bring healing. We did understand that each of us had greater faith and a deeper prayer life because Andy showed Christ's love in a handicapped body.

■ THE BIBLE LESSON

1 Now Peter and John went up together into the temple at the hour of prayer, being the ninth hour.

2 And a certain man lame from his mother's womb was carried, whom they laid daily at the gate of the temple which is called Beautiful, to ask alms of them that entered into the temple;

3 Who seeing Peter and John about to go into the temple asked an alms.

4 And Peter, fastening his eyes upon him with John, said, Look on us.

5 And he gave heed unto them, expecting to receive something of them.

6 Then Peter said, Silver and gold have I none; but such as I have give I thee: In the name of Jesus Christ of Nazareth rise up and walk.

7 And he took him by the right hand, and lifted him up: and immediately his feet and ankle bones received strength.

8 And he leaping up stood, and walked, and entered with them into the temple, walking, and leaping, and praising God.

. . . .

5 And it came to pass on the morrow, that their rulers, and elders, and scribes,

6 And Annas the high priest, and Caiaphas, and John, and Alexander, and as many as were of the kindred of the high priest, were gathered to-gether at Jerusalem.

7 And when they had set them in the midst, they asked, By what power, or by what name, have ye done this?

8 Then Peter, filled with the Holy Ghost, said unto them, Ye rulers of the people, and elders of Israel,

9 If we this day be examined of the good deed done to the impotent man, by what means he is made whole;

10 Be it known unto you all, and to all the people of Israel, that by the name of Jesus Christ of Nazareth, whom ye crucified, whom God raised from the dead, even by him doth this man stand here before you whole.

11 This is the stone which was set at nought of you builders, which is become the head of the corner.

12 Neither is there salvation in any other: for there is none other name under heaven given among men, whereby we must be saved.

■ THE LESSON EXPLAINED

Healing Draws Attention (3:1–11)

People won't listen to the gospel anymore. No matter how good the preaching is, you can't get a crowd for revivals. That's the talk we hear today. The disciples had no trouble attracting a crowd. God's power did it for them. The disciples went to pray. They met a man brought to beg. This occurred at the temple's most breath-taking entrance.

"Money to help a lame man. A few cents for bread," he cried for help. He was almost comfortable begging others for what he could not get for himself.

The disciples knew a better way. Having left their nets, their financial picture mirrored the beggars. They offered an unexpected resource: walk as you have never done in your life. You can do it. Jesus Christ has the power to make you walk. Take my hand. Come on up.

Strength has come. My ankles, my knees, my legs . . . they feel different. I can walk! I can jump! Praise the Lord, let's go pray where I have never been accepted to pray.

How could that happen? Never saw anything like it. Tell us

how such a thing can be.

Yes, God's power draws a crowd.

Preaching Explains Healing (3:12-26)

Don't look at us. We are no better than you. God did it. He wants you to know about His Son Jesus. You have heard of Him before. You sent Him to death on the cross and let a murderer go free. God raised Him back to life. Yes, Jesus whom you killed gave power for this man to walk. By faith in Jesus, he walks. I know you did not mean to kill God's Son. You did not understand what the Bible taught. Now, you have another chance, thanks to this man and his faith. Turn away from your sins. Let God erase your sins. Enjoy the salvation Jesus is bringing. Remember your alternative: destruction. God has given you first chance. Trust Jesus, and let His power work in your life as in the lame man's. He will solve your sin and guilt problem.

Testimony Offers Salvation (4:1-12)

Resurrection. That's our hot button word, yelled the Sadducees. You know Moses did not teach resurrection. Stop that foolish preaching. To jail with them.

Yours is not the only opinion, countered the crowd. What he says makes sense. You certainly can read Scripture as they do, and certainly we need help with our sins. We will believe, all 5,000 of us.

It's morning. Now we can get all our people together and teach you a lesson or two about the Bible. Listen up, disciples of Jesus. Tell us what you have been preaching.

Peter paused and knew that the Spirit was with him in this time of need just as Jesus had promised. Do you realize what you are doing? You have put us on trial for helping a man walk for the first time in his life. If that is a crime, then here is the way it happened. Jesus Christ, the one you all crucified on the cross, the one God raised from the dead, yes, Jesus provided the power for this man to walk. Let me tell you the most important point. Jesus wants to give you salvation from your sins. Only He can do it. God has not given saving power to anyone else. Will you let Jesus save you?

■ TRUTHS TO LIVE BY

Physical challenges may be doors to spiritual power. The lame man wanted money for bread. He received power to walk. More importantly he received faith in God. He traded the beggar's vocabulary for the language of praise. God remains all powerful and unselfish with His power. Have you asked Him for power recently?

Spiritual challenges may be opportunities to witness. The path to prayer became a chance to heal. Healing led to jail and the courtroom. Fear, frustration, and failure to talk were natural reactions. Only spiritually handicapped people respond that way. The disciples saw the opportunity to tell about Jesus and offer salvation. How long since you used a hard situation to point people to salvation?

Witness challenges point away from self to Jesus. Center stage fascinates us. We want to stay there as long as possible, basking in the spotlight. The disciples turned the spot light in new directions. First, on the audience. Let them see themselves as God saw them. Then on Jesus. Let the people see Him as God saw Him. Now on decision. You cannot ignore Jesus. You must go away with salvation, or you go away facing destruction. Which will it be?

■ A VERSE TO REMEMBER

The Comforter . . . whom the Father will send in my name, he shall teach you all things, and bring all things to your remembrance, whatsoever I have said unto you.—John 14:26

■ DAILY BIBLE READINGS

Sept. 11 — Commissioned to Heal and Preach. Matt. 10:1–10
Sept. 12 — A Crippled Hand Made Well. Mark 3:1–6
Sept. 13 — Sent Forth. Mark 16:9–16
Sept. 14 — Gifts from the Spirit. 1 Cor. 12:1–11
Sept. 15 — Wondrous Healing. Acts 5:12–16
Sept. 16 — Healing Explained. Acts 3:9–16
Sept. 17 — Fearless Preaching. Acts 4:13–20

Obedient to the Spirit

ACTS 5:17-32

Time for jail service. Come with us!" I can still hear Tom's invitation ringing in my ears. As a college freshman I joined the Christian student group in it's monthly jail witnessing program. I thought I had really done something for the Lord, risking my personal safety among all those criminals at the jail. Years later, traveling through eastern Europe with Christians ready to witness even in the face of enemy tanks, I learned how little I had risked for my Lord.

■ THE BIBLE LESSON

17 Then the high priest rose up, and all they that were with him, (which is the sect of the Sadducees,) and were filled with indignation,

18 And laid their hands on the apostles, and put them in the common prison.

19 But the angel of the Lord by night opened the prison doors, and brought them forth, and said,

20 Go, stand and speak in the temple to the people all the words of this life.

21 And when they heard that, they entered into the temple early in the morning, and taught. But the high priest came, and they that were with him, and called the council together, and all the senate of the children of Israel, and sent to the prison to have them brought.

22 But when the officers came, and found them not in the prison, they returned, and told,

23 Saying, The prison truly found we shut with all safety, and the keepers standing without before the doors: but when we had opened, we found no man within.

24 Now when the high priest and the captain of the temple and the chief priests heard these things, they doubted of them whereunto this would grow.

25 Then came one and told them, saying, Behold, the men whom ye put in prison are standing in the temple, and teaching the people.

26 Then went the captain with the officers, and brought them without violence: for they feared the people, lest they should have been stoned.

27 And when they had brought them, they set them before the council: and the high priest asked them,

28 Saying, Did not we straitly command you that ye should not teach in this name? and, behold, ye have filled Jerusalem with your doctrine, and intend to bring this man's blood upon us.

29 Then Peter and the other apostles answered and said, We ought to obey God rather than men.

30 The God of our fathers raised up Jesus, whom ye slew and hanged on a tree.

31 Him hath God exalted with his right hand to be a Prince and a Savior, for to give repentance to Israel, and forgiveness of sins.

32 And we are his witnesses of these things; and so is also the Holy Ghost, whom God hath given to them that obey him.

■ THE LESSON EXPLAINED

Obedience to Persecution (vv. 17–18)

Circumstances can change suddenly. Peter could not believe it. God gave the church new members faster than the church could absorb them. Every time he preached, hundreds responded. When he went to the streets, people came from everywhere wanting healing, and God healed them. Life was fantastic.

Then, oh then, the big religious boys could not take it any longer. The high priest and his Sadducee friends got really mad. They came in full force. Peter found himself escorted straight to prison. Now what? Peter knew the answer. God had been faithful in success. God would be faithful in suffering. Peter had to remain just as faithful. The Spirit who healed could also deliver from prison and deliver what was needed in prison.

Obedient to Preach (vv. 19–25)

Faithful Peter found God faithful. God's messenger invited Peter and the other apostles to follow him out of the prison and back to the streets to preach. The apostles quickly obeyed. Again they found people eagerly waiting to hear and obey their preaching and teaching.

Reaction on the other side also came as expected. The priests called their forces together. Real problems now. Could they not find a way to stop this new church from growing? Where would the end be? Would the church survive and the priesthood perish?

Self-preservation raised its head immediately. Get them back in prison immediately. No sooner said than done. Obedient apostles found themselves chained and in prison. Why? Could God not protect them? How could they obey Him any more? Perhaps they should just accept their fate, shut up, and wait until the priests' anger subsided. Perhaps they should quit preaching altogether and go back to their fishing nets or other occupations. Or did God have an opportunity for prisoners to join in His mission?

Obedient Under Persecution (vv. 26-32)

Fears haunted priests as well as apostles. Oh so quietly they went about the business of arresting the apostles. After all, this could cause a riot. People loved the apostles and the power they showed in healing, teaching, and preaching. Who knows? The people might pick up stones and protect the apostles.

Arrest accomplished. Time for trial. Call the prisoners. How dense are you guys? We gave clear instructions. No preaching. Do not mention this Jesus name. But you . . . you have filled the city with your doctrines. You have the people so turned on, they may turn on us. They blame us for killing Jesus. You must stop this.

As usual, the apostles looked to Peter to speak. And he spoke! Briefly, powerfully. Look at the choice we face. Obey you. Obey God. Which shall it be? Look at the evidence. God sent Jesus. You killed Jesus. God raised Jesus from the dead. God took Jesus up to heaven on a cloud. Jesus now is our Savior. He gives us power to repent. He forgives us. And you? What have you done for us? Put us in prison. Why? Because we preach? That is all we can see you have done.

God! We see all He has done with our own eyes. Moreover, He has put His Holy Spirit in our lives. He wants us to obey Him. He told us to preach. The more we obey, the more power He seems to give us. Now you answer. What is our choice. Obey you? Obey God?

■ TRUTHS TO LIVE BY

God expects obedience. Obedience is not a prize for a few special apostles. Obedience is not an add-on you give to God when things are going well. Obedience is a natural response to God's love in Christ. He died. He was raised. He gives salvation and forgiveness. And you? You respond in loving obedience. That is the love relationship you have with God.

God honors obedience. God reveals His presence to those who obey. The revelation may be a great escape story like the apostles in prison. It may be a great power story, like the apostles preaching and healing. It may be a great privilege story, like the apostles having the privilege to witness to the very ones trying to kill them. As God reveals His presence, He reveals His ways. Gradually, He lets you see how He responds to your obedience in ways that bring Him glory and further His mission. You see, God honors obedience rather than rewarding obedience in the way the world seeks rewards.

God deserves obedience. You may obey different people for different reasons. You obey the boss to be paid. You obey bullies to protect yourself. You obey police because you believe in law and order. You obey God because He alone deserves your obedience. He is the Creator, Redeemer, Savior, Lord. He has shown in every way possible that He loves you. He alone totally deserves your total obedience. Still He gives you the choice. You know He expects obedience . . . honors obedience . . . deserves obedience. Unlike humans, He does not force obedience. He allows you to choose. Will you obey? Are you obeying?

■ VERSE TO REMEMBER

Peter and the other apostles answered and said, We ought to obey God rather than men.—Acts 5:29

■ DAILY BIBLE READINGS

Sept. 18 — Noah's Obedience. Gen. 6:13–14,19,21; 7:5
Sept. 19 — Obedience Better Than Sacrifice. 1 Sam. 15:19–26
Sept. 20 — Pious Talk Not Enough. Matt. 7:15–23
Sept. 21 — Wise Builders. Matt. 7:24–28
Sept. 22 — To Love Is to Obey. John 14:15–23
Sept. 23 — Lying to the Spirit. Acts 5:1–12
Sept. 24 — Faithful and Counted Worthy. Acts 5:33–42

Chosen to Serve

ACTS 6:1-14

Some days live in memory forever. A conference center full of people prayed and praised. Men and women whose names filled my who's who among Christian leaders filled the platform. My wife and I joined a line of normal people like us standing in God's spotlight. God was using these people to set us apart to missionary service. We had been chosen to serve God. No idea what experiences lay ahead. Not expecting a beloved father-in-law to be dead in a year, four parents in ten years. Not knowing the turmoil foreign life would bring for children. The experiences and traumas did not matter. God had called. We had answered. We were chosen to serve.

■ THE BIBLE LESSON

1 *And in those days, when the number of the disciples was multiplied, there arose a murmuring of the Grecians against the Hebrews, because their widows were neglected in the daily ministration.*

2 *Then the twelve called the multitude of the disciples unto them, and said, It is not reason that we should leave the word of God, and serve tables.*

3 *Wherefore, brethren, look ye out among you seven men of honest report, full of the Holy Ghost and wisdom, whom we may appoint over this business.*

4 *But we will give ourselves continually to prayer, and to the ministry of the word.*

5 *And the saying pleased the whole multitude: and they chose Stephen, a man full of faith and of the Holy Ghost, and Philip, and Prochorus, and Nicanor, and Timon, and Parmenas, and Nicolas a proselyte of Antioch:*

6 *Whom they set before the apostles: and when they had prayed, they laid their hands on them.*

7 *And the word of God increased; and the number of the disciples multiplied in Jerusalem greatly; and a great company of the priests were obedient to the faith.*

8 And Stephen, full of faith and power, did great wonders and miracles among the people.

9 Then there arose certain of the synagogue, which is called the synagogue of the Libertines, and Cyrenians, and Alexandrians, and of them of Cilicia and of Asia, disputing with Stephen.

10 And they were not able to resist the wisdom and the spirit by which he spake.

11 Then they suborned men, which said, We have heard him speak blasphemous words against Moses, and against God.

12 And they stirred up the people, and the elders, and the scribes, and came upon him, and caught him, and brought him to the council,

13 And set up false witnesses, which said, This man ceaseth not to speak blasphemous words against this holy place, and the law:

14 For we have heard him say, that this Jesus of Nazareth shall destroy this place, and shall change the customs which Moses delivered us.

■ THE LESSON EXPLAINED

The Problem (vv. 1–2)

No fair! The church is not paying attention to us. They care only for people who look like they look, talk like they talk, and dress like they dress. We are going to walk out!

Wait! What do you expect? Are we supposed to quit preaching so we can serve some helpless women food every day? So the argument surged, and the church stewed. What could be done? Why had the church dared reach out to people who preferred to speak Greek rather than Hebrew? Sure, they were still Jews. Yes, Christ died for them. But they are not like us. Christ does not really expect us to get along with them! What can we do?

The Purpose (vv. 3–4)

The solution seemed easy enough—share the leadership. Let the Greek speakers choose seven people to represent the whole church in ministering to the needs of the poor widows. More leaders . . . more ministries . . . continued prayer and witnessing . . . more people satisfied. That sounds like a good purpose for our church. Find people who can do different things for God. Let God lead them to do the things they do best. Let God's church fulfill all the work God has for His church to do.

The Performance (vv. 5–8)

Beyond all expectations, these Greek-speaking leaders. The church grew by leaps and bounds. Even priests who had been putting us in prison now joined us in God's work for Jesus. And Stephen! Feed the widows. He did that well, and so much more. Every day brought a new miracle, a new testimony to how God was using Stephen. Forget the fussing. Faith has won out. God is getting glory as we share the ministry, feed the hungry bodies and the hungry souls, and watch our church grow in numbers and in faith.

The Persecution (vv. 9–15)

Immigrants can demand their fair share in the church. They can do their fair share in persecuting the church. They had their own special synagogue among the Jews in Jerusalem. They did not like to lose members to the church. So they tried to win an argument. Not against Stephen! Next idea. Arrest him. How? He has done nothing wrong. Oh, someone will witness against him. Just you wait. We will get people to charge him with what they charged Jesus—blasphemy, doing religion a new way. Done! But look at Stephen. His face shines. Only God's presence could do that.

■ TRUTHS TO LIVE BY

God has answers to your problems. Your church may prefer fighting to functioning. God has a faith way to make you forget your fights and forge ahead for Him. Will you seek His answer, or do you enjoy your problems and fights too much?

God has places for you to serve. You do not have to fret and search for something to do for God. He has equipped you with spiritual gifts. He has provided Christ's Spirit in you. He is at work in His world. He wants to show you where He is working. He invites you to join Him in His work. Will you accept His place of service?

God offers His presence while you serve. People will protest and persecute. God will choose and encourage and equip. When you accept His invitation to serve, life will change. You must make adjustments. As you do, you will experience God's presence showing His approval to your obedient service.

■ VERSE TO REMEMBER
Whom they set before the apostles: and when they had prayed, they laid their hands on them.—Acts 6:6

■ DAILY BIBLE READINGS
Sept. 25 — Willing to Serve. Ps. 40:4–10
Sept. 26 — Ready to Serve. Isa. 6:1–8
Sept. 27 — Joy in Service. Ps. 126:1–6
Sept. 28 — Shared Benefits. John 4:31–38
Sept. 29 — Christ's Example. Matt. 20:20–28
Sept. 30 — Serving Through Hardships. 1 Thess. 2:1–9
Oct. 1 — God's Reward. Eph. 6:1–8

Philip: Witness to Outcasts

ACTS 8:5-6,26-38

Bobbie was only twelve. She probably taught me, her pastor, more than all the rest of the congregation together. Bobbie lived with her abusive father and the rest of the family in a shabby tenant house. She attended school when farm duties allowed. She attended church every time she could get there. She found the joy of Jesus as our deacons and Sunday School teachers reached out to her. Her joyous, infectious faith led me to preach on witnessing to the less fortunate, gave members courage to provide food and clothes for those who needed them, and evoked love from a deacon to repair, provide electricity and plumbing for, and refurbish the tenant house Bobbie occupied. I often wonder, did I witness to an outcast, or did the social outcast witness to me?

■ THE BIBLE LESSON

5 Then Philip went down to the city of Samaria, and preached Christ unto them.

6 And the people with one accord gave heed unto those things which Philip spake, hearing and seeing the miracles which he did.

. . . .

26 And the angel of the Lord spake unto Philip, saying, Arise, and go toward the south unto the way that goeth down from Jerusalem unto Gaza, which is desert.

27 And he rose and went: and, behold, a man of Ethiopia, an eunuch of great authority under Candace queen of the Ethiopians, who had the charge of all her treasure, and had come to Jerusalem for to worship,

28 Was returning, and sitting in his chariot read Isaiah the prophet.

29 Then the Spirit said unto Philip, Go near, and join thyself to this chariot.

30 And Philip ran thither to him, and heard him read the prophet Isaiah, and said, Understandest thou what thou readest?

31 And he said, How can I, except some man should guide me? And he desired Philip that he would come up and sit with him.

32 The place of the scripture which he read was this, He was led as a sheep to the slaughter; and like a lamb dumb before his shearer, so opened he not his mouth:

33 In his humiliation his judgment was taken away: and who shall declare his generation? for his life is taken from the earth.

34 And the eunuch answered Philip, and said, I pray thee, of whom speaketh the prophet this? of himself, or of some other man?

35 Then Philip opened his mouth, and began at the same scripture, and preached unto him Jesus.

36 And as they went on their way, they came unto a certain water: and the eunuch said, See, here is water; what doth hinder me to be baptized?

37 And Philip said, If thou believest with all thine heart, thou mayest. And he answered and said, I believe that Jesus Christ is the Son of God.

38 And he commanded the chariot to stand still: and they went down both into the water, both Philip and the eunuch; and he baptized him.

■ THE LESSON EXPLAINED

The Wrong Race (8:5–8)

Half-breeds. Mixed their blood with foreigners when Assyria exiled Israel and brought outsiders in to occupy the land. Worship at the wrong place in the wrong way with the wrong Scriptures. Yes, Samaritans formed the wrong race for the Jews. But not for God. He sent Philip the deacon there to witness and work miracles. Many Samaritans ignored race as Philip and God had. They trusted Jesus and found joy.

The Wrong Faith (8:9–25)

Sorcery. Magic. The mysterious arts. There lay Simon's faith. Or did it. Maybe money formed the idol he worshiped. No matter. He surprised everyone. He joined them in believing when Philip came to preach. When Peter and John ensured everyone received the Holy Spirit, Simon wanted in on the action. The old man came back into play. He would pay money for power. That sure was the wrong faith. God and His gifts wear no price tags. Repent or perish. What do you think Simon chose now? Notice Peter and John. They chose a new course, too. They preached to the wrong race as Philip had.

The Wrong Handicap (8:26–38)

Responsible job. The nation's ruler depended on him for so much. He controlled the national treasury. He controlled many people's lives. One thing he could not control. Years ago he had chosen a handicap to gain an office. He gave up his masculinity so the queen could trust him totally. Then God took over. He lured the Ethiopian eunuch to Jerusalem and to Him. Jewish tradition took over. People handicapped as he was could not enter the temple to worship or be accepted into Judaism. He stood halfway between the religion of his country and the religion of his choice. So he returned home, riding in comfort, but reading in pain. This was Scripture, but he did not understand. Then God sent Philip. Philip showed that Isaiah 53 pointed to Jesus. Then Philip pointed the eunuch to Jesus. No physical handicap could separate him from Jesus and the church. Only sin could. The eunuch chose Jesus and showed that he did by being baptized. Another outcast joined God's incrowd.

■ TRUTHS TO LIVE BY

God wants you to understand His Word and His ways. Birth, race, cultural or religious background, physical condition . . . none of these figure in God's ways. Each person is invited to hear His Word. Each needs you to explain His Word. The Word explained and understood leads to salvation in Christ and baptism.

God wants you to forsake the world's word and the world's ways The world wants to make you special by putting others beneath you or by selling you temporary power because you have special gifts or special resources. God wants to make you special by making you His child, absolutely equal with all His other children. You do not have to buy your way into His family, nor can you buy any special position or power in His family. All is by His grace and by His choice. Is His way better for you than the world's?

God wants you to witness to His Word and His ways. God gave you all you have. Will you share Him with someone else, no matter what might seem to separate you from the other person? God will give you the opportunity and the power. Will you witness to His chosen whom the world may call outcasts?

■ A VERSE TO REMEMBER

Then Philip opened his mouth, and began at the same scripture, and preached unto him Jesus.—Acts 8:35

■ DAILY BIBLE READINGS

Oct. 2 — A Leper Cleansed. Matt. 7:24–8:4
Oct. 3 — Harlots Accepted. Matt. 21:28–32
Oct. 4 — Tax Collectors Justified. Luke 7:24–30
Oct. 5 — A Sinner Forgiven. Luke 7:36–50
Oct. 6 — Paradise Promised. Luke 23:32–42
Oct. 7 — Outcasts Brought In. Isa. 7:1–3, 10–12
Oct. 8 — Faith Generated in One Cast Out. John 9:24–38

Saul Becomes a Disciple

ACTS 9:1-6,10-20

The Russian is coming. The Russian is coming. News spread through the campus quickly. Miraculously, a student from the Soviet Union had gained permission to leave the country and study in Switzerland for four years. Now how did we respond? Would the Russians let a dedicated preacher out of the country? Or was he really a government spy using us for his purposes? Should we love and teach him, or fear and watch him?

■ THE BIBLE LESSON

1 And Saul, yet breathing out threatenings and slaughter against the disciples of the Lord, went unto the high priest,

2 And desired of him letters to Damascus to the synagogues, that if he found any of this way, whether they were men or women, he might bring them bound unto Jerusalem.

3 And as he journeyed, he came near Damascus: and suddenly there shined round about him a light from heaven:

4 And he fell to the earth, and heard a voice saying unto him, Saul, Saul, why persecutest thou me?

5 And he said, Who art thou, Lord? And the Lord said, I am Jesus whom thou persecutest: it is hard for thee to kick against the pricks.

6 And he trembling and astonished said, Lord, what wilt thou have me to do? And the Lord said unto him, Arise, and go into the city, and it shall be told thee what thou must do.

. . . .

10 And there was a certain disciple at Damascus, named Ananias; and to him said the Lord in a vision, Ananias. And he said, Behold, I am here, Lord.

11 And the Lord said unto him, Arise, and go into the street which is called Straight, and inquire in the house of Judas for one called Saul, of Tarsus: for, behold, he prayeth,

12 And hath seen in a vision a man named Ananias coming in, and putting his hand on him, that he might receive his sight.

13 Then Ananias answered, Lord, I have heard by many of this man, how much evil he hath done to thy saints at Jerusalem:

14 And here he hath authority from the chief priests to bind all that call on thy name.

15 But the Lord said unto him, Go thy way: for he is a chosen vessel unto me, to bear my name before the Gentiles, and kings, and the children of Israel:

16 For I will shew him how great things he must suffer for my name's sake.

17 And Ananias went his way, and entered into the house; and putting his hands on him said, Brother Saul, the Lord, even Jesus, that appeared unto thee in the way as thou camest, hath sent me, that thou mightest receive thy sight, and be filled with the Holy Ghost.

18 And immediately there fell from his eyes as it had been scales: and he received sight forthwith, and arose, and was baptized.

19 And when he had received meat, he was strengthened. Then was Saul certain days with the disciples which were at Damascus.

20 And straightway he preached Christ in the synagogues, that he is the Son of God.

■ THE LESSON EXPLAINED

The Church Faces the Threat (9:1–2)

The Threat. Enough said. Everyone in the church knew to whom you referred. Saul, the Jews' agent of death for the church. Now, he is coming our way, to Damascus. How can we hide? Maybe we'd better go back to the synagogue and forget Jesus. Must be some way of escape.

The Threat Faces the Lord (9:3–9)

No worry. God retains control even over the Threat. Sure, Saul started for Damascus with power to kill. God did not let him get there, for God had other plans for this dedicated young man. The Threat would be the Missionary Apostle.

Bright light. Then no light for Saul, only blindness. God got his attention. I am Jesus, the one you are trying to threaten. Hard job, isn't it? Not to worry. I have a job for you. Get into Damascus, and I will tell you more. Meantime, I have another call to make.

The Lord Faces the Mediator (9:10–16)

God came calling. Ananias answered, as usual. God's message was anything but usual. Go see the Threat. You will find him praying. He is expecting you. Now, Lord, come on. You know him as well as I do. His prayers point to my grave. Do not worry about that. He is a special case. I have invited him to be my missionary to the foreigners. You must help Me prepare him for what he has to suffer for Me.

If you say so, Lord. Here I go. Go with me.

The Mediator Faces the Convert (9:17–20)

Saul, it is Ananias. Are you really expecting me? God has something special for you.

Oh, come in. God said you would come. Please help me. I know how bad I was. I know now how good Jesus is. What can I do?

No worry. I will put my hands on you in prayer, and God will give you back your sight. See! You get something else. God is giving you His Holy Spirit. This gives you power to do His work and be like Him.

What a change. Saul could see. He wanted baptism. He had to learn everything the other believers could teach him. Then he ventured into the synagogue. No one could believe it. The Threat was the Testifier. If God can do that for him and for the church, He can do anything. I will believe, too.

■ TRUTHS TO LIVE BY

God can overcome all the threats you face. Life often looks dark. Enemies outnumber friends. Doom looms around the corner. God's Spirit resides in you. When Spirit meets threat, who will win?

God wants a love relationship with you. Your past does not matter. Saul was a murderer, enemy number one for the church. God made him missionary number one for His church. To do so, God showed Saul He loved him for who he was and could be, not for what he had been and done. God is not kicking against you. Are you kicking against Him?

God has a mission for you. God saves for service. He saves no one for idleness and uselessness. Right now He has an invitation with your name on it. It may be to be a mediator of His love and power to a special vessel in His kingdom. If you do not go, you and God's called vessel may both miss God's opportunity for service and blessing. Obey the mission; experience God.

■ A VERSE TO REMEMBER

He is a chosen vessel unto me, to bear my name before the Gentiles, and kings, and the children of Israel.—Acts 9:15

■ DAILY BIBLE READINGS

Oct. 9   — How Paul Became a Disciple. Gal. 1:11–19
Oct. 10   — Called to Preach to Gentiles. Acts 22:12–21
Oct. 11   — Benefited from Roman Citizenship. Acts 22:22–29
Oct. 12   — Plot Against Paul's Life. Acts 23:6–15
Oct. 13   — Paul Preaching in Rome. Acts 28:23–31
Oct. 14   — Paul's Care for the Church. 1 Thess. 3:1–13
Oct. 15   — Saul on the Damascus Road. Acts 9:1–9

Gentiles Receive the Spirit

ACTS 10:30-39

Olga and Ollie had the Spirit. Everyone knew it. Everyone on campus talked about it. People said they spoke in tongues. No, I do not mean a different language. Everyone on our campus spoke different languages, at least fifteen or twenty different ones. Not being able to understand what people were talking about was an everyday occurrence. But Olga and Ollie spoke a language no human had taught them. They did not tell anyone about it, especially. They did not claim to be better than I was, nor did they want to force me to be like them. They became wonderful friends. Yet, somehow, they had a gift I did not have. Was it from the Spirit? I do not have to answer that question. God knows its answer. I do have to realize different people experience God in different ways, and God wants all of them to know Him.

■ THE BIBLE LESSON

30 And Cornelius said, Four days ago I was fasting until this hour; and at the ninth hour I prayed in my house, and behold, a man stood before me in bright clothing,

31 And said, Cornelius, thy prayer is heard, and thine alms are had in remembrance in the sight of God.

32 Send therefore to Joppa, and call hither Simon, whose surname is Peter; he is lodged in the house of one Simon a tanner by the seaside: who, when he cometh, shall speak unto thee.

33 Immediately therefore I sent to thee; and thou hast well done that thou art come. Now therefore are we all here present before God, to hear all things that are commanded thee of God.

34 Then Peter opened his mouth, and said, Of a truth I perceive that God is no respecter of persons:

35 But in every nation he that feareth him, and worketh righteousness, is accepted with him.

36 The word which God sent unto the children of Israel, preaching peace by Jesus Christ: (he is Lord of all:)

37 That word, I say, ye know, which was published throughout all Judea, and began from Galilee, after the baptism which John preached;

38 How God anointed Jesus of Nazareth with the Holy Ghost and with power: who went about doing good, and healing all that were oppressed of the devil; for God was with him.

39 And we are witnesses of all things which he did both in the land of the Jews, and in Jerusalem;

■ THE LESSON EXPLAINED

The Vision (vv. 30–33)

I saw it. I know it sounds strange, but I saw it. An angel from God spoke to me. He said my prayers had been answered. The good works I had done for the Jews and other people, God had seen as evidence I was sincere in trying to please Him.

But what a way to answer prayer. I had to send my people to Joppa and find an old Jewish fisherman named Simon Peter. He would bring the answer to my prayers. What else was I to do. I had prayed. God had responded. So I obeyed. I sent my people to Joppa to find Simon (see vv. 1–8).

The Lesson (vv. 34–35)

A fierce struggle brought Peter to Cornelius. He, too, had a vision (vv. 10–16) and still had doubts (v. 17). The arrival of Cornelius' messengers helped Peter learn the lesson: God has no prejudice. He has a mission to redeem all people of all colors, races, nationalities, and locations. A redeemed person is easily spotted, for that person fears God and acts in righteousness like God.

The Word (vv. 36–43)

Peter had the answer to Cornelius' prayers. The answer was the Word. The Word was the gospel of Jesus Christ, good news of peace. The Word centered on the personal history of Jesus, the universal Lord. John the Baptist said Jesus would come. God anointed Jesus with the Spirit and with power after John baptized Him. In God's presence and power, Jesus helped people whom the evil one oppressed. Finally, the world and national powers could stand the threat no longer. They crucified Jesus. God did them one better. He raised Jesus from death and displayed Him openly to people He had chosen as witnesses. Jesus was surely alive again, for He ate and drank just as we do. Jesus had one important message for us those last days. He told us the Great Commission. He wants us to preach His Word to everyone in all the world. They must know they will die. Then they will see Him as the final Judge. We should have known that. All our prophets pointed us to Him.

You have one question, I know. How do I get ready to meet the Judge? Simple. Trust your life to Him. Believe in Him. He will forgive your sins and prepare you to meet the Judge.

The Visit (vv. 44–48)

Believe? Cornelius surely did. So did the people with Him. God showed they had believed. He sent the Holy Spirit to them. What a shock for some of the Jews. They knew God's demands. These foreigners at least had to be circumcised and agree to the Jewish law. They must be Jews before God would accept them. Did God shock them! Cornelius and his people had all the gifts of the Spirit the Jews had. Who could demand more? So Cornelius led his people into the baptismal waters.

■ TRUTHS TO LIVE BY

God has no prejudice and wants you to be like Him. God created all people and wants to redeem all people. He lives in you and wants you to be His agent to bring all people to His redemption.

God saves people through Jesus Christ. God wants you to trust in Christ for salvation, follow Him in baptism, receive the gift of the Spirit, and know the Word about Jesus well enough to tell it to others.

God will judge all people through Jesus Christ. Final judgment is a truth no human argument can get around. You and everyone you ever meet will face Jesus in the judgment. You are responsible before God to let every person know what they will face and how to face it.

God gives the Holy Spirit to His people. The Holy Spirit shows you where God is at work and how you can join Him in His work of redemption. Are you trusting God enough to let the Holy Spirit direct what you do? Or do human prejudices and fears still control the decisions you make?

■ VERSES TO REMEMBER

God is no respecter of persons: But in every nation he that feareth him, and worketh righteousness, is accepted with him.—Acts 10:34–35

■ DAILY BIBLE READINGS

Oct. 16 — Nations Blessed Through Abraham.
          Gen. 22:15–19
Oct. 17 — All Families to Worship God. Ps. 22:27–31
Oct. 18 — Israel a Light to the Nations. Isa. 49:17
Oct. 19 — All Peoples to Serve God. Dan. 7:13–18
Oct. 20 — Gentiles, Fellow Heirs. Eph. 3:1–6
Oct. 21 — Gentiles Welcomed. Rom. 15:7–21
Oct. 22 — All Are Invited. Rev. 22:12–21

The Church at Antioch

ACTS 11:19-30; 12:24-25

R evival! Billy Graham taught me the meaning of revival at a young age. My aunt took our family to Graham's Oklahoma City crusade. A vivid memory of the night is losing the location of our car and stumbling through the parking lot looking for it. A more vivid memory is joining thousands of people in dedicating myself to God's service anew and afresh and seeing God's church grow as God blessed the preaching of His Word.

■ THE BIBLE LESSON

19 Now they which were scattered abroad upon the persecution that arose about Stephen travelled as far as Phenice, and Cyprus, and Antioch, preaching the word to none but unto the Jews only.

20 And some of them were men of Cyprus and Cyrene, which, when they were come to Antioch, spake unto the Grecians, preaching the Lord Jesus.

21 And the hand of the Lord was with them: and a great number believed, and turned unto the Lord.

22 Then tidings of these things came unto the ears of the church which was in Jerusalem: and they sent forth Barnabas, that he should go as far as Antioch.

23 Who, when he came, and had seen the grace of God, was glad, and exhorted them all, that with purpose of heart they would cleave unto the Lord.

24 For he was a good man, and full of the Holy Ghost and of faith: and much people was added unto the Lord.

25 Then departed Barnabas to Tarsus, for to seek Saul:

26 And when he had found him, he brought him unto Antioch. And it came to pass, that a whole year they assembled themselves with the church, and taught much people. And the disciples were called Christians first in Antioch.

27 And in these days came prophets from Jerusalem unto Antioch.

28 And there stood up one of them named Agabus, and signified by the Spirit that there should be great dearth throughout all the world: which came to pass in the days of Claudius Caesar.

29 Then the disciples, every man according to his ability, determined to send relief unto the brethren which dwelt in Judea:

30 Which also they did, and sent it to the elders by the hands of Barnabas and Saul.

. . . .

24 But the word of God grew and multiplied.

25 And Barnabas and Saul returned from Jerusalem, when they had fulfilled their ministry, and took with them John, whose surname was Mark.

■ THE LESSON EXPLAINED

Revival Comes to God's Church (11:19–21)

How can God let this happen to us? We have done all we know. We have tried to obey Him in every way possible. Now this. We are public enemy number one. Everyone wants to kill us. We have to get out of town or be killed.

Look what God is doing! We leave town and find chances to tell people everywhere about Jesus. Look how far north and west God has spread the gospel through us. Should we thank God for persecution? He surely has used the government's evil for the gospel's good. People are turning to God everywhere. Praise God!

Maturity Comes to God's Church (11:22–26)

Revival is getting out of our control. What can we do about it? The church is no longer just in Jerusalem and where our people are. The church is scattered to the winds. Let's send representatives up to Antioch and see that everything is all right.

Yes, Barnabas can represent us. What a sight Barnabas saw. Evidence of God's grace everywhere. People certainly showed a love relationship with God in all they were doing at Antioch. God was present there. What could Barnabas do? Encourage them. Call them to maintain their close relationship to God. Show them the example of His own obedience and faith. Watch while God made the revival go on as the church matured, learning how God acted to grow His church.

Barnabas learned one thing. He could not do the Antioch work alone. He needed help. Where was Saul of Tarsus? He needed to be involved in God's revival work. Barnabas changed church history with one decision for God. He went to Saul for help in a work bigger than he was. When Saul came, the church learned even more. Their maturity showed to the world. The world called them Christians, "identified with and belonging to Christ."

Ministry Preserves God's Church (11:27–30; 12:24–25)

Mother churches never forget their missions. Jerusalem still wanted to help Antioch. They sent prophets to help the church at Antioch find where God was at work. Agabus (see 21:10) informed them that a famine would threaten the Roman Empire. This meant the poor, metropolitan, persecuted church at Jerusalem would suffer more than most. The mature church at Antioch had an immediate answer. We must help. Each member gave as much as possible. Barnabas and Saul represented the Antioch church now, sending help to the mother church in Jerusalem.

Famine came to the church. So did persecution (12:1–22). Still, God showed He maintained sovereign control of the world He created (v. 23). Famine and persecution cannot stop God and His church. The revived, mature, ministering church grew and got ready for a new step in God's work. As they grew, they continually found new leaders to guide them in growth. Crises did not matter. The church focused on what God was doing, and God worked to fulfill His mission of world redemption. A focused church and a God at work always mean a church growing and ministering.

■ TRUTHS TO LIVE BY

God is at work to bring revival to His church. God looks for leaders with dedication and vision and for a church wanting to grow and mature. He gives them His Spirit and shows them where and how He is at work. Revival comes. Is your church looking for God at work?

God wants His church to mature. God's grace constantly

works through His people, but His people must be willing to be instruments of grace. God's ministers lead the church to hold tight to God and ignore the world's threats. When God's people let His Spirit live in them and work through them, the church matures.

God guides His church to minister. God will show His church needs that the church can meet. God calls the church to use its resources to meet the needs God shows them, not to use its resources on selfish projects that bring glory to humans rather than to God. Are you and your church willing to give so you can minister?

■ A VERSE TO REMEMBER

[Barnabas] exhorted them all, that with purpose of heart they would cleave unto the Lord.—Acts 11:23

■ DAILY BIBLE READINGS

Oct. 23 — Life in the Church. Rom. 12:1–13
Oct. 24 — One Body with Many Gifts.
1 Cor. 12:12–20,27–30
Oct. 25 — Prayer for a Church. Eph. 1:15–23
Oct. 26 — The Church as a Unit. Eph. 4:1–15
Oct. 27 — Paul's Care of the Churches. 2 Cor. 12:14–21
Oct. 28 — Guidelines for Christian Conduct. Titus 3:1–11
Oct. 29 — Guidelines for Church Leaders. 1 Tim. 3:1–7

Mission to Gentiles
ACTS 13:1-5; 14:1-7,24-27

Cooped up in the little apartment with a landlord above us admitting he beat his wife, we wondered why we ever thought about being missionaries. First days of German language classes brought even more doubts. Then came Wilbur Stambaugh and Herbert Jaksteit, an English preacher and a German preacher. They shared a vision of ministry and a dedication to God. We knew then. Missions is not easy. Missions is God's way.

■ THE BIBLE LESSON

1 Now there were in the church that was at Antioch certain prophets and teachers; as Barnabas, and Simeon that was called Niger, and Lucius of Cyrene, and Manaen, which had been brought up with Herod the tetrarch, and Saul.

2 As they ministered to the Lord, and fasted, the Holy Ghost said, Separate me Barnabas and Saul for the work whereunto I have called them.

3 And when they had fasted and prayed, and laid their hands on them, they sent them away.

4 So they, being sent forth by the Holy Ghost, departed unto Seleucia; and from thence they sailed to Cyprus.

5 And when they were at Salamis, they preached the word of God in the synagogues of the Jews: and they had also John to their minister.

. . . .

1 And it came to pass in Iconium, that they went both together into the synagogue of the Jews, and so spake, that a great multitude both of the Jews and also of the Greeks believed.

2 But the unbelieving Jews stirred up the Gentiles, and made their minds evil affected against the brethren.

3 Long time therefore abode they speaking boldly in the Lord, which gave testimony unto the word of his grace, and granted signs and wonders to be done by their hands.

4 But the multitude of the city was divided: and part held with the

Jews, and part with the apostles.

5 And when there was an assault made both of the Gentiles, and also of the Jews with their rulers, to use them despitefully, and to stone them,

6 They were ware of it, and fled unto Lystra and Derbe, cities of Lycaonia, and unto the region that lieth round about:

7 And there they preached the gospel.

. . . .

24 And after they had passed throughout Pisidia, they came to Pamphylia.

25 And when they had preached the word in Perga, they went down into Attalia:

26 And thence sailed to Antioch, from whence they had been recommended to the grace of God for the work which they fulfilled.

27 And when they were come, and had gathered the church together, they rehearsed all that God had done with them, and how he had opened the door of faith unto the Gentiles.

■ THE LESSON EXPLAINED

Missions Is a Calling (13:1–5)

What a diverse crew God has put together. Niger means "black," and the church leader may be African in origin. Lucius came from northern Libya. Manaen grew up with the political leader of the province. Prayer and faith joined them when birth, race, locality, and language should have separated them. Prayer led them to see God had a great new work to do. They listened to God in prayer. They obeyed. Saul and Barnabas with John Mark became the first "foreign missionaries" a church ever sent out. The church did only what the Spirit said. When the Spirit called, the church answered, and missionaries went to preach the Word. Missionary work did not prove easy, for too many people had too many reasons not to want missionaries (see vv. 6–52).

Missionaries Lead People to Faith (14:1–7)

A strange place, strange customs, no friends. What does a missionary do? Go find religious people and start talking about Jesus. What happens? God goes to work. People respond to talk about Jesus. People believe.

Then something else happens. Unbelievers feel threatened. Their culture, their religion, their economic system, their nation has always lived one way. They want no changes, particularly not changes foreigners bring. Get rid of the foreigners. Go back to our old-time religion. But what if they have the truth? How could they? They are foreigners. They do not know what has always worked for us and what will continue to work.

How do missionaries respond to defensive opposition who take the offense against foreign missionaries? Missionaries do one thing. They preach Jesus with boldness! They talk about God's grace. They depend on God to work miracles to show He is the truth.

Opposition does not stop. What then? Eventually missionaries may have to flee the country. As they do, they leave believers behind and trust God will use them to continue the growth of His church. Wherever missionaries go, opposition follows. Missionaries have to remain true to the message and position God has given them (vv. 8–18), endure persecution (vv. 19–20), and encourage the believers (vv. 21–23).

Missionaries Report to Their Home Church (14:24–27)

Wonder whatever happened to those two young ones we sent out so long ago? Anyone ever hear from them? How are they doing in that faraway place? People at home want to know what is happening to the people whom God calls from among them and whom they support with prayers and finances. Missionaries cannot spend all the time on the mission field. They need to come back for renewal among their own people and to report to their people what God is doing around the world. A church that sends deserves to be a church that hears God's results. God's results provide further encouragement to support missions and further encouragement to find what else God is doing that the church can join in.

■ TRUTHS TO LIVE BY

God calls people and churches to join in His mission work. God shows a church and its leaders what He is doing and going to do. The Spirit leads a church to call out and support the persons God has chosen for the mission task. The church prays and gives financial support. The missionaries go where God leads them to the work He is doing.

Missionaries lead people to find salvation in Christ. Missionaries join God in His work around the world for one reason. They want people who do not know Jesus to encounter Him and experience His salvation. God is at work preparing people to hear the gospel. Missionaries preach, teach, and demonstrate the gospel in daily life. Their actions and lives join God's preparation and Spirit to bring people to salvation.

Missionaries are accountable to the church that sent them. Missionaries are not exalted people standing above all other Christians. Missionaries, like all Christians, have found God at work and have joined Him where He leads them. God leads missionaries to the field to share Jesus. He leads them back home to report on what God is doing. Church and missionaries grow and mature together as they feel responsibility to one another and as they support one another.

■ A VERSE TO REMEMBER

They . . . gathered the church together, they rehearsed all that God had done with them, and how he had opened the door of faith unto the Gentiles.—Acts 14:27

■ DAILY BIBLE READINGS

Oct. 30 — Witnessing in Cyprus. Acts 13:6–12
Oct. 31 — Witnessing in Antioch in Pisidia. Acts 13:13–25
Nov. 1 — Paul's Sermon Continues. Acts 13:26–39
Nov. 2 — Gentiles Happy. Acts 13:40–51
Nov. 3 — Mistaken Identity. Acts 14:8–18
Nov. 4 — Churches Revisited and Strengthened. Acts 14:19–23
Nov. 5 — The Christian's Loyalty. Matt. 10:34–39

The Jerusalem Conference

ACTS 15:1-2,6-18

Deacons teach pastors a lot. This young pastor felt really good about the church. Attendance was up; people were saying good things about the church; everything seemed to go well. Then a family came for church membership. I was thrilled. I had been talking to them for months. The deacons did not share the thrill. They did not think the family were sincere in requesting church membership. Pastor could not automatically win his way. Church conference had to meet and make the decision.

■ THE BIBLE LESSON

1 *And certain men which came down from Judea taught the brethren, and said, Except ye be circumcised after the manner of Moses, ye cannot be saved.*

2 *When therefore Paul and Barnabas had no small dissension and disputation with them, they determined that Paul and Barnabas, and certain other of them, should go up to Jerusalem unto the apostles and elders about this question.*

. . . .

6 *And the apostles and elders came together for to consider of this matter.*

7 *And when there had been much disputing, Peter rose up, and said unto them, Men and brethren, ye know how that a good while ago God made choice among us, that the Gentiles by my mouth should hear the word of the gospel, and believe.*

8 *And God, which knoweth the hearts, bare them witness, giving them the Holy Ghost, even as he did unto us;*

9 *And put no difference between us and them, purifying their hearts by faith.*

10 *Now therefore why tempt ye God, to put a yoke upon the neck of the disciples, which neither our fathers nor we were able to bear?*

11 But we believe that through the grace of the Lord Jesus Christ we shall be saved, even as they.

12 Then all the multitude kept silence, and gave audience to Barnabas and Paul, declaring what miracles and wonders God had wrought among the Gentiles by them.

13 And after they had held their peace, James answered, saying, Men and brethren, hearken unto me:

14 Simeon hath declared how God at the first did visit the Gentiles, to take out of them a people for his name.

15 And to this agree the words of the prophets; as it is written,

16 After this I will return, and will build again the tabernacle of David, which is fallen down; and I will build again the ruins thereof, and I will set it up:

17 That the residue of men might seek after the Lord, and all the Gentiles, upon whom my name is called, saith the Lord, who doeth all these things.

18 Known unto God are all his works from the beginning of the world.

■ THE LESSON EXPLAINED
The Controversy (15:1–5)

Belonging to the same church does not mean we agree on everything. We remain individuals with strong opinions. When you live one way all your life, you find it awfully hard to change all your opinions overnight. On the other hand, when God has struck you over the head with a truth, you find it hard to believe everyone does not understand things the way you do. Tradition opposes new understandings and experiences. How do you settle the issue?

Jerusalem settled it by bringing the parties together. Let each tell what they thought and why. We think new believers in Christ must become Jews. After all, Jesus was a Jew. He Himself said God had sent Him to the Jews. So become a Jew. Then you can become a Christian.

Oh, no, God has changed things completely. We have preached to Gentiles. They have done nothing to become Jews, but God has given them the Holy Spirit. We are not going back to tell them they have to do something else to be saved. Good enough for God; good enough for us.

All well and good, but read Scripture. Moses said to be circumcised. They must be circumcised. No other way.

The Conference (15:6–12)

Only hope for a solution rests in compromise. Bring the leaders together and find God's answer. Peter got all this started at Pentecost. What is his viewpoint? He says, You know my experience. I have told you about it often enough. God chose me to go to Cornelius and the Gentiles. I did not want to. God said, Go, in no uncertain terms. I went. God gave them salvation and the Spirit. God demanded no more. I demand no more. To do more is to become Satan and tempt God. You want them to obey a law we never have succeeded in obeying. Why? Is not God's grace in Christ enough?

Paul, you and Barnabas have a lot of experience with Gentiles. What do you say? God has done miracles among the Gentiles without demanding circumcision.

The Compromise Solution (15:13–22)

James, you are the Lord's brother. You lead the Jerusalem church where people are demanding circumcision. How can we solve this matter? Let's try it this way. You have heard Simon Peter's testimony. You know Scripture supports him. Just look at Amos 9:11–12. Christ took up the Old Testament concept of the people of God as a kingdom of priests. God has made Jesus the new Anointed One, the new Messiah, the new King. God has given Jesus a new people, the kind of people God intended all along, a people including both Gentiles and Jews, a people with one thing in common. We all believe in Jesus.

Now we see happening what the prophets promised. Jews and Gentiles are together in Christ. How do we keep us together. Here's my suggestion for compromise solution.

No circumcision. No becoming Jews. But something to mark them off from the pagan community and the Gentile gods. Eat no meat that was sacrificed to idols. Eat no meat that is strangled so that blood remains in it. Remain pure sexually unlike the pagan religious fertility rites. . . .Then the believers who feel they must maintain Jewish ties and Jewish laws can still associate with you. Let's keep the fellowship but not make burdens we cannot keep and God does not demand. These four demands are not too hard for anyone to follow. They allow you to associate with and witness to both Jews and Gentiles. Is that a fair solution? Sure it is! Thank God. Again He has worked among us to keep the church together and to keep mission witness to all people alive and flourishing.

■ TRUTHS TO LIVE BY

The church faces problems. God's salvation does not isolate the church from problems human personalities and relationships create. Problems are not the trouble. Failure to find God's solution is. God will work through dedicated leaders to find a way that both parties can agree on and that helps fulfill God's mission among both groups.

Discussion and witness lead to solutions. God is working in His church. Let people testify to what God is doing. Let the Holy Spirit use the evidence of what God is doing in His church to lead you to a solution that is God's way of continuing to work among all people in His church.

Compromise may be God's way. You cannot go into a problem-solving conference convinced you have all the truth. You go searching to find where and how God is working. Then you ask God to show you the way that can maintain your witness among your group while helping the other group maintain its witness, too. God may expect life adjustments from both groups so He can continue working best to redeem all persons in all the world.

■ A VERSE TO REMEMBER

We believe that through the grace of the Lord Jesus Christ we shall be saved, even as they.—Acts 15:11

■ DAILY BIBLE READINGS

Nov. 6 — Difficulty of Keeping the Law. John 7:14–24
Nov. 7 — Justification by Faith. Gal. 2:11–21
Nov. 8 — Forgiveness of Sins. Acts 10:39–43
Nov. 9 — Righteousness Bestowed by Christ. Isa. 53:7–12
Nov. 10 — Approval for Jerusalem. Acts 15:19–29
Nov. 11 — Letter Received with Rejoicing. Acts 15:30–41
Nov. 12 — Grace for All. Rom. 3:21–31

A Gospel Unhindered by Geography
ACTS 16:9–10,13–15,25–34

One May Day that almost forced us to scream, May Day, May Day. God had given us the opportunity to teach in Yugoslavia. Why the schedule called for travel on the communists' major holiday, I will never know. Try to find the right bus and then the right hotel when all the signs are written in a foreign alphabet. Then tell a taxi driver you want to go to Voy Vodina. Yes, that is the name of the hotel. It is also the name of everything else in the place, for it is the name of the state. Then find you and your wife have a single room reserved. Almost makes you wish missionary service had geographical limits.

■ THE BIBLE LESSON

9 And a vision appeared to Paul in the night; There stood a man of Macedonia, and prayed him, saying, Come over into Macedonia, and help us.

10 And after he had seen the vision, immediately we endeavored to go into Macedonia, assuredly gathering that the Lord had called us for to preach the gospel unto them.

. . . .

13 And on the sabbath we went out of the city by a river side, where prayer was wont to be made; and we sat down, and spake unto the women which resorted thither.

14 And a certain woman named Lydia, a seller of purple, of the city of Thyatira, which worshiped God, heard us: whose heart the Lord opened, that she attended unto the things which were spoken of Paul.

15 And when she was baptized, and her household, she besought us, saying, If ye have judged me to be faithful to the Lord, come into my house, and abide there. And she constrained us.

. . . .

25 And at midnight Paul and Silas prayed, and sang praises unto God:

and the prisoners heard them.

26 And suddenly there was a great earthquake, so that the foundations of the prison were shaken: and immediately all the doors were opened, and everyone's bands were loosed.

27 And the keeper of the prison awaking out of his sleep, and seeing the prison doors open, he drew out his sword, and would have killed himself, supposing that the prisoners had been fled.

28 But Paul cried with a loud voice, saying, Do thyself no harm: for we are all here.

29 Then he called for a light, and sprang in, and came trembling, and fell down before Paul and Silas,

30 And brought them out, and said, Sirs, what must I do to be saved?

31 And they said, Believe on the Lord Jesus Christ, and thou shalt be saved, and thy house.

32 And they spake unto him the word of the Lord, and to all that were in his house.

33 And he took them the same hour of the night, and washed their stripes; and was baptized, he and all his, straightway.

34 And when he had brought them into his house, he set meat before them, and rejoiced, believing in God with all his house.

■ THE LESSON EXPLAINED

A Vision Beyond Boundaries (16:9–12)

Where next? We have completed the task here. God's church is planted and at work. How do we know what to do next? Let's take a survey. Let's look at demographic statistics. Let's see where our plan says to go next. Remember, we have a five-year program we have to follow. What about a revolutionary idea? Why not ask God where He is at work and wants us to work? Paul got a surprise. Get out of Asia Minor. I want you on the other side of the Aegean Sea in Macedonia. That works. Ask God where He is working. Listen until He answers. Then obey.

God Gives Converts in New Territories (16:13–15)

What do we do when God sends us into unfamiliar territory? Same thing we have always done for Him. Find people at worship and tell them about Jesus. Of course, this is strange. Only women are worshiping. Dare we men approach them? Did God send you here to do His work? Preach the gospel. What do you expect to happen? One of the leading women believes, leads her family to believe, calls for baptism to show her faith to everyone there, and makes her house the missionaries' headquarters. That is God's way. Find where He is at work. Testify of what Jesus has done for you. Expect God to make converts to the gospel and supply your needs.

New Territory May Mean New Prisons (16:16–24)

Yours is not the only religious business in town. Other people find that religion is quite a profitable business. They do not want competition. Paul provided competition for people making a living off a young lady possessed by a demon. The Greeks thought she represented the god Apollo. As usual, the demon knew the truth and so led the young lady to proclaim exactly who Paul and the other missionaries were (v. 17). Paul knew God did not need this kind of witness, so he called the demon out of the girl. The result: punishment and prison.

God Delivers from All Troubles (16:25–34)

How do you react to prison? With praise, of course. God heard the praise and the prayers. He sent an earthquake. The prison opened. Good news for prisoners. Terrifying news for jailers, news calling for suicide. Paul had good news, even for the jailer. Prisoners had not taken advantage of the situation. His job was safe.

Now the jailer knew a higher kind of deliverance. He had heard the prayer and praise. He knew Paul's God was greater than anything he had experienced. How could he find salvation for eternity? Paul told him simply: Believe on Christ. He did. So did his family. Paul preached. They were baptized. Salvation had come in a foreign prison. God can surely bring salvation and deliverance to anyone, anywhere. What a reason for praise and joy!

■ TRUTHS TO LIVE BY

God has a plan to spread the gospel. Do we spend too much time planning and not enough praying and preaching? God has a plan to spread His Word and wants to share the plan with you and your church. Ask Him.

God's work is bringing people to salvation. He wants to save people where you are through your witness. He will lead you to opportunities to witness. Will you let Him? Ask Him.

God overcomes everything that hinders salvation. You do not have to provide salvation. You do not have to win arguments. God can defend Himself. He wants you to present your testimony about Jesus. He wants you to invite Him to work through you. Obey, and experience God at work overcoming obstacles to salvation.

God's salvation brings joy. Do you want joy for yourself, your family, and others? Accept God's salvation. Tell others about it. Watch God bring joy.

■ A VERSE TO REMEMBER
After he had seen the vision, immediately we endeavoured to go into Macedonia, assuredly gathering that the Lord had called us for to preach the gospel unto them.—Acts 16:10

■ DAILY BIBLE READINGS
Nov. 13 — Solving a Mother's Need. Exod. 2:1–10
Nov. 14 — God's Response to His People's Cry. Exod. 3:1–8
Nov. 15 — Caring for a Fellow Traveler. Luke 10:25–37
Nov. 16 — The Spirit's Response to Our Cry. Rom. 8:12–17
Nov. 17 — Timothy Enlisted as Helper. Acts 16:1–8
Nov. 18 — Arrested for Helping a Slave Girl. Acts 16:16–24
Nov. 19 — Released for Continued Ministry. Acts 16:35–40

Power of the Gospel

ACTS 19:1–6,11–20

J im Williams may have been the most capable student I ever taught. As a student he wrote papers I encouraged him to submit for publication to scholarly journals. Jim married a dedicated young woman from Yugoslavia. With potential to do graduate work and teach in places around the world, Jim listened to God rather than to his teachers. He went with his wife to teach in Yugoslavia, where Christian teachers were and are rare. He wrote Greek and other teaching tools in the Serbo-Croatian language that they had never had before. A tragic accident took his young life, but the few years he lived illustrated to all of us the power of the gospel to control and transform lives. People from at least four continents still look back twenty years to the power Jim had and continues to have on our lives.

■ THE BIBLE LESSON

1 And it came to pass, that, while Apollos was at Corinth, Paul having passed through the upper coasts came to Ephesus: and finding certain disciples,

2 He said unto them, Have ye received the Holy Ghost since ye believed? And they said unto him, We have not so much as heard whether there be any Holy Ghost.

3 And he said unto them, Unto what then were ye baptized? And they said, Unto John's baptism.

4 Then said Paul, John verily baptized with the baptism of repentance, saying unto the people, that they should believe on him which should come after him, that is, on Christ Jesus.

5 When they heard this, they were baptized in the name of the Lord Jesus.

6 And when Paul had laid his hands upon them, the Holy Ghost came on them; and they spake with tongues, and prophesied.

. . . .

11 And God wrought special miracles by the hands of Paul:

12 So that from his body were brought unto the sick handkerchiefs or aprons, and the diseases departed from them, and the evil spirits went out of them.

13 Then certain of the vagabond Jews, exorcists, took upon them to call over them which had evil spirits the name of the Lord Jesus, saying, We adjure you by Jesus whom Paul preacheth.

14 And there were seven sons of one Sceva, a Jew, and chief of the priests, which did so.

15 And the evil spirit answered and said, Jesus I know, and Paul I know; but who are ye?

16 And the man in whom the evil spirit was leaped on them, and overcame them, and prevailed against them, so that they fled out of that house naked and wounded.

17 And this was known to all the Jews and Greeks also dwelling at Ephesus; and fear fell on them all, and the name of the Lord Jesus was magnified.

18 And many that believed came, and confessed, and showed their deeds.

19 Many of them also which used curious arts brought their books together, and burned them before all men: and they counted the price of them, and found it fifty thousand pieces of silver.

20 So mightily grew the word of God and prevailed.

■ THE LESSON EXPLAINED

The Missing Power (19:1–5)

Everything is fine with me. I believe in God. He has saved me. I have nothing else to fear, nothing else to wish for. Wait a minute. Take an inventory. What do you have? Are you missing something? These questions Paul had to raise, for he met deceived believers. They thought John had the final word. Paul said, No, only Jesus has the final word. If you do not have the power of the Holy Spirit, a power only Jesus can give, then you are missing power.

The Rejected Power (19:6–9)

Faith brings salvation. Salvation brings the Spirit. The Spirit brings power through spiritual gifts. Faith does not, however, force.

You can reject the power. Even Paul could not persuade everyone to believe. Many rejected his witness. He took that for three months and then left the premises. God refuses to continue working where people reject Him and His power.

The Accepted Power (19:10–12)

Faithful witness does not meet total rejection. Many accept your witness and thus accept God's power. Then what happens? The good news spreads far and wide. Those who hear take the news to those who do not know. Miracles happen. When people accept God's power, God shows just how powerful He is.

The Counterfeit Power (19:13–20)

If Paul can do that, why can't I? I will listen closely and act just as he does. One problem. The power is not in Paul. The power is not in magic words. The power is not in imitation. The power is in God. You cannot counterfeit God, so you cannot counterfeit His power. Those who try quickly find this out. Some Jews could use the strangeness of their language, culture, and religious ways to fool the overly religious Greeks. They had nothing to use to fool Paul and Paul's God. The power of evil took over them when they tried to take over God's power in counterfeit ways.

Counterfeiting God's power brought positive results. Fear of God flowered. No one else gave in to the temptation to counterfeit. Many listened to the testimony of Paul and others and found the true power. This power did two things. It gave them power to do miracles (v. 18) and courage to forsake totally all fake avenues to power (v. 19). Now the Word showed its power (v. 20), for God prevails over all counterfeits and substitutes.

■ TRUTHS TO LIVE BY

Salvation in Jesus brings the power of the Spirit. Do you lack spiritual power? Do you never know what God wants you to do? Prayer time! Confess your faith in Christ, and ask for His Spirit to work His power in your life.

Rejecting God's power means losing life's hope. God wants to love you in Christ and give you power to face life's toughest situations. He will not force you to accept His power. You must trust Him.

Alternate power sources do not exist. It is God's power or nothing. You choose all power or no power: God in you or a huge vacancy sign on your heart.

■ A VERSE TO REMEMBER

So mightily grew the word of God and prevailed.—Acts 19:20

■ DAILY BIBLE READINGS

Nov. 20 — Leader of Synagogue Converted. Acts 18:1–11
Nov. 21 — Apollos Strengthens Believers. Acts 18:24–28
Nov. 22 — Idolatry Threatened by the Gospel. Acts 19:21–34
Nov. 23 — Order Restored by Clerk's Logic. Acts 19:35–41
Nov. 24 — Paul's Thanksgiving and Confidence. Rom. 1:8–17
Nov. 25 — The Spirit's Power in Christ. Luke 4:14–21
Nov. 26 — Power to Give Eternal Life. John 17:1–5

A Time of Comfort
ISAIAH 40:1-11

American jets have just shot down two American helicopters as I write this lesson. Twenty–six people died. Just as Operation Desert Storm was blowing into the pages of history and off the minds of our people, tragedy renews all the old hurts, griefs, and losses. Individuals, families, and a nation join again in grief. As tears flow, anger rises, and frustration explodes. Where do we turn for help?

God's prophet faced a similar situation. He had to prepare a people to endure exile and ignore squashed hopes for release. Suddenly, he changed his tune. He found a new message, a message of comfort for a grieving, angry, frustrated people. Strangely, people ignored the message of comfort as easily as they had ignored earlier messages of judgment. Will you listen as God seeks to bring comfort? Will you let Him bury your anger, grief, and frustration with His good news?

■ THE BIBLE LESSON

1 Comfort ye, comfort ye my people, saith your God.

2 Speak ye comfortably to Jerusalem, and cry unto her, that her warfare is accomplished, that her iniquity is pardoned: for she hath received of the Lord's hand double for all her sins.

3 The voice of him that crieth in the wilderness, Prepare ye the way of the Lord, make straight in the desert a highway for our God.

4 Every valley shall be exalted, and every mountain and hill shall be made low: and the crooked shall be made straight, and the rough places plain:

5 And the glory of the Lord shall be revealed, and all flesh shall see it together: for the mouth of the Lord hath spoken it.

6 The voice said, Cry. And he said, What shall I cry? All flesh is grass, and all the goodliness thereof is as the flower of the field:

7 The grass withereth, the flower fadeth: because the spirit of the Lord bloweth upon it: surely the people is grass.

8 The grass withereth, the flower fadeth: but the word of our God shall stand forever.

9 O Zion, that bringest good tidings, get thee up into the high mountain; O Jerusalem, that bringest good tidings, lift up thy voice with strength; lift it up, be not afraid; say unto the cities of Judah, Behold your God!

10 Behold, the Lord God will come with strong hand, and his arm shall rule for him: behold, his reward is with him, and his work before him.

11 He shall feed his flock like a shepherd: he shall gather the lambs with his arm, and carry them in his bosom, and shall gently lead those that are with young.

■ THE LESSON EXPLAINED

Call to Comfort (vv. 1–2)

Forward march! So comes God's call to you as you turn from Isaiah 39 to Isaiah 40. You must fast forward through 150 years of history, from Hezekiah in 701 B.C. to Israel's exiled prisoners of war in Babylon in 545 B.C. Assyria has vanished as a world power. Babylon will soon fall to Persia and King Cyrus, who will rule the world. God has prepared His people for this. How? As God usually does. He called a person to bring His message and call His people to join Him in His work.

The messenger had one word: Comfort. Would people listen? They had many words for God. You can read them in the Book of Lamentations. Was God fair? Just? Interested? Dead? Where was God to let His people suffer pain, loss, and humiliation? Over forty years in exile showed where God was, didn't it? Could He be anywhere but in captivity Himself, a prisoner of Babylon and Persia?

God's call to the prophet sought to change that perspective. God was alive and in charge. The work His people had done in foreign labor camps was complete. They had fulfilled the law, paying the price of their sins (see Exod. 22:1,7,9). God was ready to forgive their sins and start over. You see, Babylon did not have them captive. God did. Persia could not free them. God would.

The Revelation Reported (vv. 3–5)

How do you react when God speaks? Keep the message to

yourself so you will be one up on everyone else? Certainly not. God gives a message to share with His people. So the prophet preached. No longer must he harden hearts (ch. 6). Now he highlighted hope. God had a construction project underway, a highway of hope: "This imitated Babylonian practices in which a highway was built for the great religious festivals so that the images of the gods could be paraded before the people. Yahweh's highway was not to show off his beautiful artwork and clothing. It was to deliver his people in a moment of historical crisis" (Trent C. Butler, "Isaiah," *Layman's Bible Book Commentary 10* [Nashville: Broadman Press, 1982], 89). Israel could march from Babylon to Jerusalem in comfort on God's direct route: all obstacles eliminated.

Why would God do this? Nations laughed at Him because His people had no power. Laughter would cease. God's glory would shine. The whole world would see. "How can we be sure?" exiles in Babylon asked. Simple. God said so. Case closed.

Personal Problem for the Prophet (vv. 6–8)

God's news is so good until . . . it becomes my news. God had more than information for the prophet. He had a job assignment. Cry out the message of comfort so all will hear. Wait! That puts me in peril. My reputation is at stake. You have been silent forty years, God. Why would people listen to me, now? Go ahead and build your highway. Bring salvation. Let me enjoy it. But a job assignment for me? I am just like all other people, as lasting and meaningful as spring grass that burns up and dies in the summer heat. And, God, you are the cause. You blow with your Ruach (your breath, your Spirit, your wind) and destroy us all. Why bother with good news no one will hear and no one can do anything about?

Out of focus! That's your problem, prophet of Mine. You look at people to get your perspective. Look unto Me. I am the Source of comfort. My Word is always true and never dies or disappears. When I have spoken, you must speak, for the people need to hear My Word!

The Content of Comfort (vv. 9–11)

I can't do it alone, cries the prophet. I know, answers God.

Send it down the chain of command. The people in exile constantly call for return to Zion. Tell them to take the message to Zion, to my city Jerusalem. The message is simple: God is coming. That is the content of comfort. If God comes to you, all is well. God's presence is your only need in grief, war, frustration, anger, bad times. You want power? God brings His strength. You want direction? God will rule. You want payback for all your troubles? God comes with His reward. You want sustenance for body and soul? The Good Shepherd brings food for His sheep. You seek love? God is love and will hug you to Himself. God the Comforter comes when you need Him. Will you receive His comfort?

■ TRUTHS TO LIVE BY

You need comfort. You, like all people, are fragile as grass. Death, economic loss, job loss, children gone astray, relationships broken. You need comfort.

Comfort comes in God's time. Your task is to recognize your need and cry out for help as Israel cried. You cannot decide how and when comfort comes. That is God's decision. You must wait and trust.

Comfort comes in the personal presence of God. You may describe comfort in many different human ways. God describes comfort in only one way—I am with you always, even until the end of the world.

Comfort calls for you to accept Him. You may want something else besides God's presence. If so, you are looking to the wrong source for comfort. Comfort in time of trouble has only one source. Will you accept Him and the way He brings comfort? If so, He will call you to comfort others as a messenger of His presence.

■ A VERSE TO REMEMBER

Comfort ye, comfort ye my people, saith your God. Speak ye comfortably to Jerusalem.—Isaiah 40:1–2

■ DAILY BIBLE READINGS

Nov. 27 — Short-sighted Behavior. Isa. 39:1–8
Nov. 28 — Declaration of Sin. Mic. 3:1–8
Nov. 29 — Prayer for Blessing on the King. Ps. 72:1–14
Nov. 30 — The Appeal of Good Tidings. Isa. 52:1–10
Dec. 1 — The Lord Will Restore. Isa. 49:1–10
Dec. 2 — Gift of Abundant Life. John 10:1–11
Dec. 3 — Prayer for Deliverance. Ps. 86:8–17

A Time of Encouragement
ISAIAH 51:1-8

Courtroom . . . lawyers . . . judge . . . me. Yes, I have stood in the courtroom a few times for various reasons. None bring back fond memories. Two sides, each trying to prove the other is lying. Accusations, judgments, penalties, ruined lives, bleak futures. Color courtrooms dark for me.

Israel felt much the same. They took God to court. They demanded that some judge pronounce God guilty of child abuse. He had promised His people so much. Now they struggled as war prisoners in a foreign land, and they had done so for forty years. Where was the God of Abraham, Isaac, and Jacob? Where were the promises of land, descendants, fame as a nation, and blessing? How could pious, God-fearing people be so mistreated? Take God to court! Make Him pay what He promised!

■ THE BIBLE LESSON

1 Hearken to me, ye that follow after righteousness, ye that seek the Lord: look unto the rock whence ye are hewn, and to the hole of the pit whence ye are digged.

2 Look unto Abraham your father, and unto Sarah that bare you: for I called him alone, and blessed him, and increased him.

3 For the Lord shall comfort Zion: he will comfort all her waste places; and he will make her wilderness like Eden, and her desert like the garden of the Lord; joy and gladness shall be found therein, thanksgiving, and the voice of melody.

4 Hearken unto me, my people; and give ear unto me, O my nation: for a law shall proceed from me, and I will make my judgment to rest for a light of the people.

5 My righteousness is near; my salvation is gone forth, and mine arms shall judge the people; the isles shall wait upon me, and on mine arm shall they trust.

6 *Lift up your eyes to the heavens, and look upon the earth beneath: for the heavens shall vanish away like smoke, and the earth shall wax old like a garment, and they that dwell therein shall die in like manner: but my salvation shall be forever, and my righteousness shall not be abolished.*

7 *Hearken unto me, ye that know righteousness, the people in whose heart is my law; fear ye not the reproach of men, neither be ye afraid of their revilings.*

8 *For the moth shall eat them up like a garment, and the worm shall eat them like wool: but my righteousness shall be forever, and my salvation from generation to generation.*

■ THE LESSON EXPLAINED

Listen to History (vv. 1–3)

God went to court with Israel and took the witness stand. Who do you think you are? He asked. Righteous people who follow My teaching? Good people who seek Me and My way of life? Let's test that theory. What evidence can you put forward? Yes, you want to talk about Abraham and all I promised Him in Genesis 12. That is a good starting point. Look at Abraham, the beginning point of your national history. Look at his wife Sarah, the mother of your nation. What do you learn?

I called Abraham. He answered. I promised to bless Abraham. He went where I directed. They began as one family. I blessed. I increased. Now Abraham and Sarah live on in you, tens of thousands of people. Abraham's lesson: listen and obey. You have a whole history to look. Abraham had no history to look at. I called Abraham. He followed. I am calling you to follow Me out of exile and back to Jerusalem. Will you learn Abraham's lesson? If so, life's greatest joy awaits.

Listen to God's Promises (vv. 4–6)

The call to obedience, to join God in His work, is not enough. You want more promises. God gives promises. Promise is His game. Listen closely.

I have an action plan. I am sending My teaching or Law (Hebrew, *Torah*) , and my legal judgment (Hebrew, *mishpat*) I am proclaiming to the world. This will give light to the nations. They will know how to act. They will realize they must deal justly with you, My people. They will learn that I am bringing salvation to the world. They will trust Me. Is that encouragement enough? You want more. Look around you. Take one last look. The world vanishes. Its inhabitants all die. My salvation is the world's final word. It lasts forever. So do My righteous acts establishing justice. Complain no more. I have the world's last word. That word is hope.

Listen Without Fear (vv. 7–8)

Why do you cringe like cowards in the corner? My people, have you let adversity defeat you? Do you trust the enemy's power more than My promises? You know My righteous acts. You know My teaching. You are My people. Fear not. I will do what I promised. Human words make no difference. They cannot hurt you. I am on your side. They will die and have their cadavers eaten up. My righteous acts of salvation will protect you. You have no reason to be afraid. Stand up and look for My salvation. I promised it. Salvation comes. Are you ready?

■ TRUTHS TO LIVE BY

God's encouragement has its foundation in history. Bible hope and promise is not idealistic dreaming. It is the testimony built by generations of experience. From Abraham to Joseph to David to Isaiah to Malachi to Jesus to Paul to John to Augustine to Luther to Wesley to Martin Luther King, Jr., to you, the experiences keep coming. God gives encouraging promises. God fulfills those promises. You have reason for encouragement.

God's encouragement rests on God's acts. You do not have to rely on your power. You do not have to be on the right political side. Trust God. He acted in the past. He promises to act in the future. Trust Him and wait. Encouragement comes now. Salvation comes shortly.

God's encouragement brings justice. God's encouragement brings more than momentary deliverance from trouble. God's encouragement promises a new world order. God will establish His law for all people. All will obey. All will be righteous and just. Then trouble cannot come again. That is true encouragement.

■ A VERSE TO REMEMBER

My salvation shall be for ever, and my righteousness shall not be abolished.—Isaiah 51:6

■ DAILY BIBLE READINGS

A Time of Joy

ISAIAH 9:1-7

Define joy. Words cannot do it, can they? No, dictionary definitions bring knowledge. Joy brings emotions. Only human experiences can give meaning to joy. Weddings, births, deliverance, return home, victory, class reunions, love. You can put experiences with each of these words. Those experiences define joy. At least sometimes you can.

Days do come when joy vanishes. No memories seem to bring that special emotional feeling of hope, satisfaction, and anticipation. Then what do you do? That was Israel's question for God. God gave His prophet an answer.

■ THE BIBLE LESSON

1 *Nevertheless the dimness shall not be such as was in her vexation, when at the first he lightly afflicted the land of Zebulun and the land of Naphtali, and afterward did more grievously afflict her by the way of the sea, beyond Jordan, in Galilee of the nations.*

2 *The people that walked in darkness have seen a great light: they that dwell in the land of the shadow of death, upon them hath the light shined.*

3 *Thou hast multiplied the nation, and not increased the joy: they joy before thee according to the joy in harvest, and as men rejoice when they divide the spoil.*

4 *For thou hast broken the yoke of his burden, and the staff of his shoulder, the rod of his oppressor, as in the day of Midian.*

5 *For every battle of the warrior is with confused noise, and garments rolled in blood; but this shall be with burning and fuel of fire.*

6 *For unto us a child is born, unto us a son is given: and the government shall be upon his shoulder: and his name shall be called Wonderful, Counselor, The mighty God, The everlasting Father, The Prince of Peace.*

7 *Of the increase of his government and peace there shall be no end, upon the throne of David, and upon his kingdom, to order it, and to establish it with judgment and with justice from henceforth even forever. The zeal of the Lord of hosts will perform this.*

■ THE LESSON EXPLAINED

Joy Needed (vv. 1–2)

Israel, the northern kingdom, desperately needed joy. In 732 B.C. Assyria had annexed the northeastern corner (tribe of Naphtali) and the northwestern corner (tribe of Zebulun) of Israel's promised land. In such a time, God spoke to a prophet. Using "the Assyrian geographical divisions—'way of the sea, land beyond the Jordan, Galilee of the nations'—(v. 1)—the prophet depicted a new glory." (Butler, "Isaiah," *LBBC* 10, 37). Light replaces darkness, bringing hope where death reigned.

Joy Provided (vv. 3–5)

What brings joy? Israel had a quick answer: victory and fertility. God promised both. The nation would multiply in numbers, prestige, and influence.

(Note: Some Hebrew text does not say this will increase joy, but other Hebrew readings say this will increase joy to Israel. Most modern translators follow the more positive reading.)

How can you describe this coming joy? The experience of a marvelous crop yielding food beyond all expectations or the joy of dividing the spoils after victory in war. Name the most glorious experience you have ever had. That is the joy God promises to bring and more.

How will God bring victory? By defeating the enemy just like He defeated the Midianites in Judges 7:22–25. Warfare, its weapons and wounds, will vanish as if burned in a fire. Now that is joy. But God has more to come.

Joy in a Person (vv. 6–7)

God dressed His joy promise in a birth announcement. The birth announcement had two audiences with a view to two births. The prophet delivered the announcement to Israel's king, Ahaz. The king refused Isaiah's political advice, and the prophet promised doom to the king at the hand of Assyria (ch.7). At the same time, the prophet had pointed to a God-given son. Again in chapter 9, the prophet tells the king about a son, probably the king's own who would become the good king Hezekiah and see God deliver him from Assyria in 701 B.C. (chs. 37–39). The prophet also delivered the birth announcement to the people Israel, igniting expectations of the ultimate Messiah who would bring eternal salvation. The virgin Mary brought forth this Son, fulfilling all the hopes roused by Isaiah 7 and Isaiah 9.

God provided special names for His special Son. These descriptive titles represented the people's expectations of a king, expectations each king tried to fulfill and expectations each failed to fulfill. Only Christ Jesus showed these expectations in person.

This King shouldered all responsibility for government. He devised plans and counsel too wonderful for humans and possible only because God counseled the King (see 2 Sam. 16:23). The King could be called a mighty God because He represented God on earth before the people (see Ps. 45:6). At His coronation ritual, God adopted the King as the Son of God (Ps. 2:7; compare 2 Sam. 7:14; Ps. 89:26–27). Finally, the new King would be the Everlasting Father of the country, serving the one Eternal Father and not the temporary master, Assyria. The goals for such a King? Unlimited growth and prosperity (v. 7).

Joy in person meant more than titles. It brought responsibility. The new King would bring peace and justice to the world. This would last forever. Too good to be true? No, for the jealous, zealous God has promised. The question is not, will it happen? The question is, will you believe? If you will believe, your joy will be established (see Isa. 7:9).

■ TRUTHS TO LIVE BY

Joy comes in hopeless situations. Experiencing the darkness lends depth to the moment when joy comes. Escape from darkness shows God is at work, making the joy have lasting effect. Your day is never so dark that God cannot bring joy. Trust Him. Joy is on the way.

Joy comes to destroy your burdens. No enemy power can overpower God. He knows your situation. He already has an action play to bring joy. Wait for Him. Joy is on the way. Burdens will vanish.

Joy comes in Jesus. True joy is always personal. None of the world's glittering objects and materials can bring joy. They may hide sadness for a brief moment. God has a birth announcement for you. The Babe of Bethlehem is coming. He has a birthday present for you: joy.

■ A VERSE TO REMEMBER

For unto us a child is born, unto us a son is given: and the government shall be upon his shoulder: and his name shall be called Wonderful, Counselor, The mighty God, The everlasting Father, The Prince of Peace.—Isaiah 9:6

■ DAILY BIBLE READINGS

Dec. 11 — Suffering Servant Serves Others. Isa. 50:4–10
Dec. 12 — Oppressors Defeated. Isa. 10:20–27
Dec. 13 — God's Love Declared. John 3:16–21
Dec. 14 — Messiah Reigns as King. Jer. 23:1–6
Dec. 15 — Name Is Wonderful. Judg. 13:15–20
Dec. 16 — All Authority. Matt. 28:11–18
Dec. 17 — He Is Our Peace. Eph. 2:11–18

A Time of Righteousness and Peace

ISAIAH 11:1-6; LUKE 2: 10-14

Does war rule the world? As I write, newspaper headlines tell of killing and fighting in Rwanda, Bosnia, Israel, and in most of America's cities. Even on this Christmas Eve as you study this lesson, your newspapers probably only change the names a little. The verbs remain the same. What causes wars? Do you have hope for peace?

■ THE BIBLE LESSON

1 *And there shall come forth a rod out of the stem of Jesse, and a Branch shall grow out of his roots:*

2 *And the spirit of the Lord shall rest upon him, the spirit of wisdom and understanding, the spirit of counsel and might, the spirit of knowledge and of the fear of the Lord;*

3 *And shall make him of quick understanding in the fear of the Lord: and he shall not judge after the sight of his eyes, neither reprove after the hearing of his ears:*

4 *But with righteousness shall he judge the poor, and reprove with equity for the meek of the earth: and he shall smite the earth with the rod of his mouth, and with the breath of his lips shall he slay the wicked.*

5 *And righteousness shall be the girdle of his loins, and faithfulness the girdle of his reins.*

6 *The wolf also shall dwell with the lamb, and the leopard shall lie down with the kid; and the calf and the young lion and the fatling together; and a little child shall lead them.*

. . . .

10 *And the angel said unto them, Fear not: for, behold, I bring you good tidings of great joy, which shall be to all people.*

11 *For unto you is born this day in the city of David a Savior, which is*

Christ the Lord.

12 And this shall be a sign unto you; Ye shall find the babe wrapped in swaddling clothes, lying in a manger.

13 And suddenly there was with the angel a multitude of the heavenly host praising God, and saying,

14 Glory to God in the highest, and on earth peace, good will toward men.

■ THE LESSON EXPLAINED

The Roots of Righteousness (Isa. 11:1–3)

One wish. What do you ask? Isaiah said, a righteous leader. In so doing, he mocked and rejected the ruling king and all his family. Conditions had become so bad that God would start over again. Micah said back to Bethlehem (Mic. 5:2). Isaiah said, back to the stump left from Jesse's family tree. A new beginning, a new baby, a new hope.

How could this become reality? God's Spirit would accomplish it. The Spirit would create a new kind of ruler, unlike any Israel had known. Wise, understanding, able to counsel, powerful, intelligent, God-fearing . . . such would be God's new leader. Yet he would not depend on human skills and abilities. He would depend on God's righteousness!

The Results of Righteousness (Isa. 9:4–6)

When God provides a new ruler and the ruler depends on God for righteousness, results astonish. Earth's "little people" attract all the attention. Righteousness cares not for the rich and famous but the poor and impoverished. Any who cause injustice and poverty also attract attention; indeed, they attract attack. Righteousness routs the wicked. God's ruler wraps himself in God's righteousness and makes faithfulness the only trademark displayed on his clothes.

A righteous ruler brings astounding results even in the world of nature. Fear, fighting, and feasting on one another disappear even among battling beasts. "Natural enemies would feed together. A lad would surpass even the wildest childhood dreams, becoming king of the jungle. Human power, alone, could not accomplish this.

The holy mountain, where God resided, provided the center. From there, personal acquaintance with Yahweh, the God of Israel, would flood out over the entire world" (Butler, "Isaiah," *LBBC* 10, 1982, 43). That is God's job description for a world ruler, His picture of Israel's Messiah.

The Reality of Righteousness (Luke 2:10–14)

God's ruler of righteousness is not just a vision, a dream for the unrealized future. That Ruler came to earth, the baby Isaiah had pictured in 7:14 and 9:6. God renewed His birth announcement to the poorest of the poor, shepherds on the hillside protecting filthy, ignorant sheep. What's happening? they wondered as God's angel and glory filled the skies.

No reason to fear, came the angelic answer. You are the first to know of God's first Christmas present, a present of joy. A little baby is born, a baby with a mission. He is your Savior, your Messiah, your Lord. You can see Him in the manger in Bethlehem, David's city.

Are we dreaming? Is it real? Look, the sky is full of angels. They chorus out good news: glory for God and peace for people. What more could we ask? Let us go and see.

Yes, God's righteousness and peace are more than pious, pretty words. They became real in the not-so-peaceful setting of a cow's stall behind an overbooked inn as people crowded to pay taxes to a hated government. They became real on a Roman cross as government and religion made an unlikely alliance to crucify Bethlehem's Babe of Promise. They become real as He becomes Lord of your life. They become real as He rules the world and brings His kingdom. They become real as you seek righteousness for the poor and justice for the ignored.

■ TRUTHS TO LIVE BY

Righteousness and peace are God's goals. From Eden to eternity God works to bring peace and righteousness among people. Promising the Messiah and sending Jesus to Bethlehem are two steps in God's action plan for world peace and righteousness. Have you found your place in His action plan?

Righteousness and peace come as you care. Righteousness and peace are not nice sounding words waiting for the sweet by-and-by to become real. They become real as you cast aside selfishness and greed. They become real as you care for the uncared for. They become real when you ensure justice and hope for those without a home, without a counselor, without a dream, without hope.

Righteousness and peace are assured because Jesus came. God has given concrete proof He will succeed in achieving His goal. Jesus' ministry, death, and resurrection guarantee that. What is not sure? Your participation in His peace. That assurance comes only as Jesus is Lord and Savior of your life. Let the Babe of Christmas be born in your life and give you new birth today.

■ A VERSE TO REMEMBER

The wolf also shall dwell with the lamb, and the leopard shall lie down with the kid; and the calf and the young lion and the fatling together; and a little child shall lead them.—Isaiah 11:6

■ DAILY BIBLE READINGS

Dec. 18 — No Love, No Kinship. 1 John 4:1–12
Dec. 19 — Love Perfected. 1 John 4:13–21
Dec. 20 — Memory with Hope. Gen. 9:8–17
Dec. 21 — Immanuel, God with Us. Isa. 7:10–17
Dec. 22 — Preparation of Zechariah. Luke 1:5–17
Dec. 23 — Announcement to Mary. Luke 1:26–36
Dec. 24 — A Marvelous Birth. Luke 2:1–9

A Time for Sharing Good News

ISAIAH 60:1-4; 61:1-4

Devastation. Unforgettable. Yesterday shopping in the mall with my college son. Today, a roofless, useless mall. Tornadoes interrupted business as usual. We learned who is in control. Amid the confusion, good news. No one hurt. Everyone survived. So what do you report? Newspapers emphasize devastation.

Israel faced a similar situation. They returned to Jerusalem full of hope. God had delivered on His promises. Then reality check: temple, business, homes destroyed. Other people occupying land they claimed. How would they react? How would you?

■ THE BIBLE LESSON

1 *Arise, shine; for thy light is come, and the glory of the Lord is risen upon thee.*

2 *For, behold, the darkness shall cover the earth, and gross darkness the people: but the Lord shall arise upon thee, and his glory shall be seen upon thee.*

3 *And the Gentiles shall come to thy light, and kings to the brightness of thy rising.*

4 *Lift up thine eyes round about, and see: all they gather themselves together, they come to thee: thy sons shall come from far, and thy daughters shall be nursed at thy side.*

. . . .

1 *The Spirit of the Lord God is upon me; because the Lord hath anointed me to preach good tidings unto the meek; he hath sent me to bind up the brokenhearted, to proclaim liberty to the captives, and the opening of the prison to them that are bound;*

2 *To proclaim the acceptable year of the Lord, and the day of vengeance of our God; to comfort all that mourn;*

3 *To appoint unto them that mourn in Zion, to give unto them beauty*

*for ashes, the oil of joy for mourning, the garment of praise for the spirit
of heaviness; that they might be called trees of righteousness, the planting
of the Lord, that he might be glorified.*

*4 And they shall build the old wastes, they shall raise up the former
desolations, and they shall repair the waste cities, the desolations of
many generations.*

■ THE LESSON EXPLAINED

God's Glory: The Source of Good News (60:1–4)

Frustrated returned exiles found God had left a word for
them. Stand up and get ready for duty. God's good news is just
started with the return from Babylon. You will get to see all His glory, that is "the weighty importance and shining majesty which ac-
company God's presence . . . . that side of God which humans
recognize and to which humans respond in confession, worship,
and praise" (*Holman Bible Dictionary*, Holman Bible Publishers,
1991, 557). Are you ready for that privilege? Realize, that all other
nations must live in darkness. You alone have God's glory to give
light and direction. Such light will attract unbelieving Gentiles.
They will come to you to worship your God and to bring back your
exiled family from around the world. Are you ready to tell them,
your enemies, about God when they come?

Gentile Gold: The Resources for Good News (60:5–22)

Self-pity consumed Israel. They resided in the promised land
but without promised resources: no money, no homes, no temple,
no political power. Never fear, came God's good news. I will attract
the Gentiles. They will bring the resources you need. They will also
come to worship your God. You can use the offerings the Gentiles
bring to rebuild My house in all its glory. Then you, too, will have
glory.

How can all this be? Is God fickle? God said He sent us to exile
because we sinned against His covenant. Now suddenly He brings
all this good news. What are we supposed to think about Him?

Oh, no! I am constantly pursuing a love relationship with
you. My anger and punishment is discipline done in love trying
to bring you back to Me. With discipline over, I now bring news

of mercy and love. Will you respond in trust and commitment? Will you tell others the good news? I will defeat all your enemies and bring them to serve you and Me.

Why do I do this? The same reason I have always worked for you. I want you and the world to know I alone am God, the Savior and Redeemer. I am all you need. You do not even need sun and moon. My brilliant glory will be your light source. You will be obedient, righteous. You will inherit the promised land forever. Tell the good news!

God's Spirit: The Power for Good News (61:1–4)

So He brings good news, grand-sounding promises. What do you do about it? You let the Spirit lead you. He has a commission for you. God is working to bring hope and justice to the poor. The Spirit sends you to do the same. Tell people what God has promised and trust Him to do it when He chooses. Mourning and grief, wishing and complaining are no longer in order. Sharing God's good news is. Tell others. Live like the righteous God. Then you will bring glory to God and find Him making good news real.

Jesus took this one step farther. He made the Spirit's commission His commission (Luke 4:16–21). He called you to follow Him in accepting that same commission. Will you?

■ TRUTHS TO LIVE BY

Good news can be preached in bad times. God does not limit the call to preach good news to people enjoying "good times." He has shown you His salvation. He calls you to share the news with others, especially the underprivileged.

Good news gives God glory. Sharing good news is the Spirit's commission to you. The purpose is to lead people to a saving relationship with God. That brings glory to God, not to you. Do you love God enough to do what brings God glory and ignore your own glory?

Good news is directed to all people, even your enemies. God does not call you to be selective in how you share good news. He calls you to share the good news with unbelievers, different social classes, different races, different nations. Any limits you feel as to the people with whom you can share good news, you set. God has no limits. He sends you into all the world (Matt. 28:19–20). Go!

■ A VERSE TO REMEMBER

The Spirit of the Lord GOD is upon me; because the LORD hath anointed me to preach good tidings unto the meek; he hath sent me to bind up the brokenhearted, to proclaim liberty to the captives, and the opening of the prison to them that are bound.— Isaiah 61:1

■ DAILY BIBLE READINGS

Dec. 25 — Heavenly Choir. Luke 2:13–20
Dec. 26 — A Bright Future. John 6:43–47
Dec. 27 — The Glory of Christ. 2 Cor. 8:16–24
Dec. 28 — Receive Your Brother. Philem. 10–18
Dec. 29 — Honest Reasoning. Luke 5:1–10
Dec. 30 — Forsake All. Luke 5:11–15
Dec. 31 — God's Glory in Evidence. Isa. 60:15–22

The Servant's Call

ISAIAH 42:1-9

E. J. held no office in the church. Often he could not attend services, for he had to work from 6 a.m. to 11 p.m. many days. Few people did more for the church. Kids needed transportation? E. J. found a way to provide it. Church needed food for an occasion? E. J. provided it. Members down on their luck needed a bit of food to get by? Mysteriously food appeared at their door. Young pastor needed information about the community? E. J. showed where I could find that information.

No church office could define E. J., but the Bible did have a term for him—servant of the Lord.

■ THE BIBLE LESSON

1 Behold my servant, whom I uphold; mine elect, in whom my soul delighteth; I have put my spirit upon him: he shall bring forth judgment to the Gentiles.

2 He shall not cry, nor lift up, nor cause his voice to be heard in the street.

3 A bruised reed shall he not break, and the smoking flax shall he not quench: he shall bring forth judgment unto truth.

4 He shall not fail nor be discouraged, till he have set judgment in the earth: and the isles shall wait for his law.

5 Thus saith God the Lord, he that created the heavens, and stretched them out; he that spread forth the earth, and that which cometh out of it; he that giveth breath unto the people upon it, and spirit to them that walk therein:

6 I the Lord have called thee in righteousness, and will hold thine hand, and will keep thee, and give thee for a covenant of the people, for a light of the Gentiles;

7 To open the blind eyes, to bring out the prisoners from the prison, and them that sit in darkness out of the prison house.

8 I am the Lord: that is my name: and my glory will I not give to an-

other, neither my praise to graven images.

9 Behold, the former things are come to pass, and new things do I declare: before they spring forth I tell you of them.

■ THE LESSON EXPLAINED

The Servant Introduced (vv. 1–4)

God's people needed help. They begged God for a new king, a David who would restore their political power and pride. God's ways are not human ways. He selected a servant, not a king. He challenged Israel to accept servant leadership and to imitate their leader. Carefully God described His way of human servant leadership. He depended on God's strength, not human strength. He delighted God, not people. He depended on God's Spirit not on human power structures. He worked quietly, refusing to cry out and call attention to himself or to hurt anything. Still, quiet confidence would characterize him, and he would succeed.

What is success for him? the people wondered. God had a one-word answer: judgment or justice (Hebrew, *mishpat*, vv. 1,4). What is that? No English word describes it. "In verse 4 it stands parallel to Torah, law or teaching. It is the verdict handed down by a judge (2 Kings 25:6); the whole court process (Isa. 3:14); the gracious and merciful judgment of God (Isa. 30:18); or the natural right and order claimed by a person or group of persons (Exod. 23:6; Isa. 10:2; 40:27)" (Butler, *LBBC 10*, 93–94). For the servant, mishpat included God's discipline on Israel and judgment on the nations, establishing a new international order of peace, justice, and stability. God would give the servant power to bring mishpat, a power exercised silently and selflessly.

The Servant's Master (vv. 5–6)

How can such a weakling succeed? We need a ruler, not a servant. Do not forget. The servant has a Ruler, a Master. This is the servant of the Lord. Look not to the servant's power. Look to the Master's power. He created this whole universe. He controls what the earth produces. He is the source of life for all people in every country. He has given the servant a special power, the power of righteousness. He can do God's righteous, saving acts that will create justice. He will make God's covenant love relationship with people a reality, bringing all nations into that covenant. Do not worry about the servant's power. Focus on God's power. Then you will want to be the servant.

The Servant's Task (vv. 7–9)

How is the servant going to do this? What action plan does God have for him? God is quite clear on the task the servant must accomplish. In fact God used three other servant songs (49:1–6; 50:4–9; and 52:13–53:12) to describe the task fully. The servant concentrated on the people God constantly concentrates on: those obviously needing help in a society that tends to ignore them, the poor, ill, blind, imprisoned. Working with these people, the servant can succeed only by depending on God. Depending on God means giving God alone the honor, glory, and praise. No substitutes for God can possibly receive credit God deserves. No other person, no material resources, no idols will receive praise. Only the servant's Master.

Sounds awfully good. How can we be sure this will work? The world does not work this way. That is the point. This is God's way, not human ways. What God has promised in the past has always come true. So will this. Will you be God's servant? In Israel God found few takers. The world's way proved too alluring. Finally, God's Son, Jesus, came to show what a Servant of the Lord could accomplish (Matt. 12:17–21). He called you to serve as He served. Will you serve Him? If not, you will serve the world, the way that never has worked.

■ TRUTHS TO LIVE BY

God calls servants, not masters, to join Him in His work. The world shoves you into the spotlight. God loves you into backstage tasks. No one may see you, but God will. A committed servant asks no more.

God seeks justice, not victory. The world calls you to defeat someone. God calls you to stoop and help someone. The world sends you to the front line. God sends you to the back streets.

God makes you a covenant minister, not a crown pre-

tender. The world sets the throne as the only worthy goal. God occupies the throne and sends you as His ambassador to lead the nations to a covenant love relationship with Him. Can you sacrifice personal power and visibility for God's blessing?

■ A VERSE TO REMEMBER

Behold my servant, whom I uphold; mine elect, in whom my soul delighteth; I have put my spirit upon Him: he shall bring forth judgment to the Gentiles.—Genesis 42:1

■ DAILY BIBLE READINGS

Jan. 1 — Song of Victory. Isa. 42:10–17
Jan. 2 — Israel—Deaf and Blind. Isa. 42:18–25
Jan. 3 — Israel's Redemption. Isa. 43:1–7
Jan. 4 — Israel, the Lord's Witness. Isa. 43:8–13
Jan. 5 — God as Redeemer. Isa. 43:14–21
Jan. 6 — The Greatness of His Power. Eph. 2:1–10
Jan. 7 — Jesus' Power. Matt. 12:22–32

The Servant's Mission

ISAIAH 49:1-6

Novi Sad, Yugoslavia. Horrible hotel. Alone. Afraid. Why would God put me in this situation? Then I listened to the seminary president who had invited me to come and teach. Yes, it is hard here. The communist government puts restrictions on us. We certainly cannot evangelize the way you do in Europe or America. But we do not use the opportunities we have. Pray for us that we will be better servants of God and evangelize our country. If they were not making the most of their opportunities, what about me? You?

■ THE BIBLE LESSON

1 Listen O isles, unto me; and hearken, ye people, from far; The Lord hath called me from the womb; from the bowels of my mother hath he made mention of my name.

2 And he hath made my mouth like a sharp sword; in the shadow of his hand hath he hid me, and made me a polished shaft; in his quiver hath he hid me;

3 And said unto me, Thou art my servant, O Israel, in whom I will be glorified.

4 Then I said, I have labored in vain, I have spent my strength for nought, and in vain: yet surely my judgment is with the Lord, and my work with my God.

5 And now, saith the Lord that formed me from the womb to be his servant, to bring Jacob again to him, Though Israel be not gathered, yet shall I be glorious in the eyes of the Lord, and my God shall be my strength.

6 And he said, It is a light thing that thou shouldest be my servant to raise up the tribes of Jacob, and to restore the preserved of Israel: I will also give thee for a light to the Gentiles, that thou mayest be my salvation unto the end of the earth.

■ THE LESSON EXPLAINED

The Servant's Call (vv. 1–3)

Woe? Alas, poor pitiful us!·So thought Israel in exile in Babylon. No one suffered as they had to suffer. No one ever had it so bad. Foreign country. Foreign gods. Foreign language. Foreign culture. Foreigners with all the power. Do something, God.

God did. He turned them to His Word. His messenger rose to retell his call experience from God. God was not silent. He had spoken. Even before the messenger was born! He equipped the messenger, giving him sword-sharp words to cut the complainers hearts and souls. Then God showed His mystery. He hid the servant in His hand, waiting for the right moment of revelation. First, He named the servant. The servant is Israel!

What? Impossible. Poor us. No power or hope. You must be fooling. Tell someone else they are God's servants.

The Servant's Complaint (v. 4)

God's messenger agreed. That is how I reacted, too. I told God, my whole life's work is meaningless, vain, chaos. I have accomplished nothing. I cannot be your servant. God had the answer. You are just like all the complaining people I call, like Moses (Exod. 3:11,13; 4:1,10), like Gideon (Judg. 6:13,15,17,22,36,39), like Jeremiah (Jer. 1:6). God finally taught me something, Israel. He showed me that He is the Judge. He will make the judgment in my case. He is in charge of the work I do and the reward I receive. God shut my complaining. He wants to shut your complaining, too.

The Servant's Commission (vv. 5–6)

Okay, you win. God had the idea of Israel as a people before the nation was born. His commission to Abraham (Gen. 12:1–7) and to Moses (Ex. 19:4–6) should be our commission. But it has not worked out like that. God lost the battle of Jerusalem in 587 B.C.; Babylon won. We cannot fulfill our commission.

You just do not get the picture, do you? Israel has a mission to Israel. Yes, you heard right. God has divided His people Israel into two groups: servant Israel and sinner Israel. Obey the commission; be Israel the servant. Otherwise, be Israel the sinner.

And the commission? Two parts: turn Israel the sinner into Israel the servant. Then get ready for action. You can do more than that. Be God's servant to the nations. Bring salvation to the whole world. Yes, in your pitiful condition in exile, win the victory over your victors. Lead them to the Lord.

■ TRUTHS TO LIVE BY

God calls you to mission. You do not rule on qualifications or opportunities. God has had a purpose for you since before you were born. The question is not, did I hear the call right? God could not mean that. The question is, will I accept God's call and join Him where He is at work?

God answers all your complaints. You the complainer join a long line of people who know they cannot do what God calls them to do. God calls only to God-sized tasks. God supplies power for the task. Mysteriously, God chooses to do the task through you. Will you let Him?

God's commission lies beyond your imagination. Thus, you know God designed the commission. You would never challenge yourself to make an impact on the entire universe. God wants you to. God will give light to the world through you. Are you content to hide in darkness and self-pity?

■ A VERSE TO REMEMBER

I will also give thee for a light to the Gentiles, that thou mayest be my salvation unto the end of the earth.—Isaiah 49:6

■ DAILY BIBLE READINGS

Jan. 8 — God Is Everywhere. Ps. 139:7–14
Jan. 9 — God Is All-Knowing. Ps. 33:12–22
Jan. 10 — God Is All-Powerful. Jer. 32:17–22
Jan. 11 — The Source of Mercy. Ps. 130:1–8
Jan. 12 — The Promise of Peace. Isa. 26:1–8
Jan. 13 — Message of Salvation. Isa. 48:9–16
Jan. 14 — Message of Joy. Isa. 48:17–22

The Servant's Steadfast Endurance

ISAIAH 50:1-11

Eighty years old. Long widowed. Left with two sons with great mental challenges, neither able to provide for himself, both over sixty years of age. Outside observers would say Grace lived in a cloud of darkness with no reason to smile. Yet hers was the home you went to for encouragement. Her smile brightened each Sunday morning as she brought the two sons to church to praise God for His blessings. God had endured with her for eighty years. She would gladly endure with Him as long as He let her.

■ THE BIBLE LESSON

4 *The Lord God hath given me the tongue of the learned, that I should know how to speak a word in season to him that is weary: he wakeneth morning by morning, he wakeneth mine ear to hear as the learned.*

5 *The Lord God hath opened mine ear, and I was not rebellious, neither turned away back.*

6 *I gave my back to the smiters, and my cheeks to them that plucked off the hair: I hid not my face from shame and spitting.*

7 *For the Lord God will help me; therefore shall I not be confounded: therefore have I set my face like a flint, and I know that I shall not be ashamed.*

8 *He is near that justifieth me; who will contend with me? let us stand together: who is mine adversary? let him come near to me.*

9 *Behold, the Lord God will help me; who is he that shall condemn me? lo, they all shall wax old as a garment; the moth shall eat them up.*

10 *Who is among you that feareth the Lord, that obeyeth the voice of his servant, that walketh in darkness, and hath no light? let him trust in the name of the Lord, and stay upon his God.*

11 *Behold, all ye that kindle a fire, that compass yourselves about with sparks: walk in the light of your fire, and in the sparks that ye have kin-*

dled. This shall ye have of mine hand; ye shall lie down in sorrow.

■ THE LESSON EXPLAINED

The Case Against God (vv. 1–3)

Your honor, the defense wishes to place the defendant on the stand. He will answer the charges of having divorced His wife and abandoned His children. Please listen to Yahweh, the God of Israel.

Your honor, I am Yahweh, the God of Israel. I am the One who rescued them in Egypt and established them as a nation through the plagues and the dividing of the Red Sea. I am the One who has brought the dark clouds today because all nature is in mourning for the plight of My people Israel. Your honor, I have not divorced them or sold them or abandoned My children. I know the law. I created the law. Divorce (Deut. 24:1–4) or child abandonment to pay debts (Ex. 21:7–11; see 2 Kings 4:1) would forfeit all My rights. The burden of proof is on Israel. Do they have divorce papers? Do they have a bill of sale where I sold My children? Of course not! They are guilty. Their trouble is My discipline for their sins. Accuse them, not Me.

The Confession of the Servant (vv. 4–9)

Friends, may I present the servant of the Lord in concert? He will give his personal testimony in poetry and song.

Thank you. I pattern my testimony on the song of confidence you know so well from Psalms 4; 11; 16; 23; 27; 62; 125; 131. You know gifts God gave me: teaching, counseling. Each new morning God wakes me up, and we share together. Thus, each day I can share in your troubles. God gives me a mission. I go to it and do not turn back.

Easy? Never! I have suffered persecution just like you, maybe more. Shameful what they put me through. My reaction? Trust God. Face the enemy stone-faced. Feel no shame because I have obeyed God. Shame would come only if I denied Him. He is my Defense Attorney. I challenge anyone to come forward, accuse me, and convict me. God will not let them. I am with God for the long run. They will wear out like a suit of clothes. I will persevere for God is with me.

The Call to Trust (vv. 10–11)

Your honor, please bring the audience to the stand. I want to question them. You have heard the commission of God's servant (chaps. 42; 49). You know God has called you to be His servant. All right! Who has obeyed? I know you say you would if God would just give you special light. He does not work that way. He simply wakes you each morning to give you light for the day. That way you must trust and depend on Him each day. Who is doing that?

No! You are not doing that? Then you face the sentencing. God will catch you in your own firetrap. You have played with fire. You will be burned. What a sorrowful sentence when you could be a saving servant.

■ TRUTHS TO LIVE BY

God remains in the salvation business. You can bring no charges against God. He is innocent of all. He has remained faithful to His commission. He is at work redeeming the world. Have you joined Him in His work? Do you trust Him to work through you?

God provides the resources you need. Your strength and resources are never enough to do God's calling. He gives you what you need to do what He leads you to do each day. Will you turn to Him each day to find the work He is doing and to receive the resources to do it.

God protects in time of trouble. God protects in trouble, not always from trouble. Can you face shame, mocking, and rejection from the world? Trust Him. Then you can. He is your Defense Attorney, too.

God expects obedience. God's expectations are high. He never sets low goals for you. He calls to perfect obedience. You cannot obey in your strength. Trust Him. He gives power to obey. Or He gives judgment.

■ A VERSE TO REMEMBER

For the Lord God will help me; therefore shall I not be confounded: therefore have I set my face like a flint, and I know that I shall not be ashamed.—Isaiah 50:7

If you prefer a "Sanctity of Life" lesson, you will find it in the back of this book.

■ DAILY BIBLE READINGS

Jan. 15 — God's Historical Faithfulness. Isa. 49:7–13
Jan. 16 — God Does Not Forget. Isa. 49:14–18
Jan. 17 — God's Restoration. Isa. 49:19–26
Jan. 18 — God Reaches Out to All People. Isa. 56:1–8
Jan. 19 — God Against Idolatry. Isa. 57:1–13
Jan. 20 — God Ready to Heal. Isa. 57:14–21
Jan. 21 — Kindness Is Better Than Fasting. Isa. 58:1–14

The Servant's Victory

ISAIAH 52:13–53:12

Victory? Or defeat? I am not sure. A long year devoted night and day to one project. Now all ready to publish and see how God can use it to change people's lives. The manager is not happy. He does not think the project meets its goals. We may not publish it at all! A year's labor destroyed? Perhaps from a human standpoint. Maybe that is how God works. How can He bring victory from the world's defeat?

■ THE BIBLE LESSON

1 Who hath believed our report? and to whom is the arm of the Lord revealed?

2 For he shall grow up before him as a tender plant, and as a root out of a dry ground: he hath no form nor comeliness; and when we shall see him, there is no beauty that we should desire him.

3 He is despised and rejected of men; a man of sorrows, and acquainted with grief: and we hid as it were our faces from him; he was despised, and we esteemed him not.

4 Surely he hath borne our griefs, and carried our sorrows: yet we did esteem him stricken, smitten of God, and afflicted.

5 But he was wounded for our transgressions, he was bruised for our iniquities: the chastisement of our peace was upon him; and with his stripes we are healed.

6 All we like sheep have gone astray; we have turned every one to his own way; and the Lord hath laid on him the iniquity of us all.

. . . .

10 Yet it pleased the Lord to bruise him; he hath put him to grief: when thou shalt make his soul an offering for sin, he shall see his seed, he shall prolong his days, and the pleasure of the Lord shall prosper in his hand.

11 He shall see of the travail of his soul, and shall be satisfied: by his knowledge shall my righteous servant justify many; for he shall bear their iniquities.

■ THE LESSON EXPLAINED
God's Reversal (52:13–15)

(Note: This is Isaiah's most important passage and probably his most difficult to understand. Pray through each word; read several translations; look at all available commentaries and helps).

What is success in God's kingdom? Living in exile in Babylon without power or temple? No! That is experiencing God's discipline for your sin. Success is being God's servant wherever He places you.

That astonishes me. The Servant of God meets no success criteria. The Servant is ugly, scarred, unhuman, horrifying!

Still, He will affect international history. He will reverse the world's fortunes in ways you never expected. Kings cannot speak until the Servant speaks. He will change all their plans. Wait and see!

The World's Refusal (53:1–3)

God works through the Servant. Who recognizes it? Certainly we have not. We have looked for strength, power, beauty, success. He is normal, not handsome, not appealing. People naturally reject Him and ignore Him. We do the same. Such a frail person has no chance to make a difference for us. We will hide. Maybe He will go away. If the world hates Him so much, why should we place any value in Him?

The Servant's Role (53:4–9)

Can you believe it? We try to escape His presence. He is doing everything we need. We thought God was punishing Him. Instead, He is taking over our griefs and sorrows. He is scarred with wounds our sins caused. We have peace and health because He suffered. We must confess. We are the sinners. Not He. Still, He suffered for us. And He never said a word. He endured a mock trial and was sentenced to death. We did not even send a reporter to see what was going on. He died as a criminal. We were guilty. We are the sinners.

They buried Him with the enemy, not even giving Him proper last rites. But He did not deserve any of this. What can this mean?

God's Renewal (53:10–12)

This means God has been at work. We would not be His servants. He found One who would. God caused all this to happen. God accepted His suffering and death as an offering for our sins, even without a temple to offer sacrifices.

What? Death is not the end. God will renew His life. God will give Him His reward after all. We multitudes will receive justice and salvation because He did not. Yes, that is God's Word. God has placed Him atop the list of world heroes when we put Him at the bottom of the list of scoundrels. We are sinners. He suffers. He dies. We are saved. We live with Him forever.

Yes, that is God's Word for the servant. When we would not be the servant, God sent One who would. His Son. Jesus is the Suffering Servant who saves you.

■ TRUTHS TO LIVE BY

God defines victory, not the world. Your success criteria do not work in the real world of eternity. God's do. They measure what you do to help people find eternal salvation from the wages of sin. What kind of victory do you seek?

God wins victory through Christ's suffering. We refused to be God's servants. He sent His Son to suffer as His servant for our sins. The cross is God's victory symbol. Now He calls you to take up the cross as the suffering servant. Are you playing on the winning team?

God's victory brings God's reward. What victory prize do you expect? The Servant suffered and was mocked, ignored, rejected, crucified. He trusted God had eternal reward. Is that victory for you?

■ A VERSE TO REMEMBER

He shall see of the travail of his soul, and shall be satisfied: by his knowledge shall my righteous servant justify many; for he shall bear their iniquities.—Isaiah 53:11

■ DAILY BIBLE READINGS

Jonah Flees from God
JONAH 1:1-2:10

Preach Jonah, Daddy. Preach Jonah. The excited ring of my boys' voices still rings in my ears. When professor Dad got invited to preach, the boys wanted to hear Jonah again. They liked to laugh at a prophet who heard God say go east and so purchased a ticket to the farthest western resort, at a prophet sleeping while pagan sailors prayed, at a thanksgiving prayer from a big fish's belly, at a five-word sermon bringing the world's greatest spiritual awakening, and at a pouting prophet bawling God out for sending revival. Jonah is a funny story. It is a sad commentary on us as people of God. While God tries to carry on a love relationship with the world, we selfishly seek to limit His love to us and to the people we like.

■ THE BIBLE LESSON

1 Now the word of the Lord came unto Jonah the son of Amittai, saying,

2 Arise, go to Nineveh, that great city, and cry against it; for their wickedness is come up before me.

3 But Jonah rose up to flee unto Tarshish from the presence of the Lord, and went down to Joppa; and he found a ship going to Tarshish: so he paid the fare thereof, and went down into it, to go with them unto Tarshish from the presence of the Lord.

4 But the Lord sent out a great wind into the sea, and there was a mighty tempest in the sea, so that the ship was like to be broken.

. . . .

10 Then were the men exceedingly afraid, and said unto him, Why hast thou done this? For the men knew that he fled from the presence of the Lord, because he had told them.

11 Then said they unto him, What shall we do unto thee, that the sea may be calm unto us? for the sea wrought, and was tempestuous.

12 And he said unto them, Take me up, and cast me forth into the sea; so shall the sea be calm unto you: for I know that for my sake this great tempest is upon you.

13 Nevertheless the men rowed hard to bring it to the land; but they could not: for the sea wrought, and was tempestuous against them.

14 Wherefore they cried unto the Lord, and said, We beseech thee, O Lord, we beseech thee, let us not perish for this man's life, and lay not upon us innocent blood: for thou, O Lord, hast done as it pleased thee.

15 So they took up Jonah, and cast him forth into the sea: and the sea ceased from her raging.

. . . .

17 Now the Lord had prepared a great fish to swallow up Jonah. And Jonah was in the belly of the fish three days and three nights.

. . . .

2:1 Then Jonah prayed unto the Lord his God out of the fish's belly,

. . . .

10 And the Lord spake unto the fish, and it vomited out Jonah upon the dry land.

■ THE LESSON EXPLAINED

Mission 1: Save Sinful Enemies (1:1–2)

Jonah is a book of mission. It contrasts God's eternal mission of redeeming a lost world and humanity's ongoing mission of self-preservation. God used Jonah in a successful mission (2 Kings 14:25). Then, as normal, God called him to an even larger, truly God-sized task: preach to the most cruel enemy on earth.

Mission 2: Escape from God (1:3–17)

Lord, You know I love You, but faith has limits. I will go anywhere You send me, but not to Nineveh. Lord, it's dangerous. Lord, we have many people here at home that need ministry. Lord, Nineveh does not deserve Your word. Lord, go ahead and destroy them. You do not have to send me. It's time for vacation. Call again when I come back and You have a better mission.

Not so fast, Jonah. You cannot escape Me. I will just pick up this wind and throw it in your face.

What do you do when God threatens you? The ship gave up and started to break in pieces. Jonah went to sleep. Pagan sailors threw away their wage-earning cargo and prayed. The rugged ship captain demanded that the prophet pray. God gave revelation to the sailors, not the prophet. The prophet spoke, but only to give name, rank, and serial number and admit he was escaping God. Finally, the prophet gave the solution: kill me. The sailors had too much human kindness. They worked harder. They prayed for mercy. Finally, they sacrificed Jonah to the storm. And then God stopped the storm. The sailors sacrificed to Jonah's God and made promises to Him. God sent a special fish for Jonah.

Mission 3: Thank God from a fish's belly (2:1–10)

What do you do when you try to escape but God finds you? Jonah cried from the realm of death and darkness (2:2; Hebrew, *Sheol*). He admitted God had directed even the fish and the chaotic waters to deliver him. From death's door, he looked forward to God's house (v. 4). He concluded his prayer as Israel always concluded thanksgivings, with a promise to offer special sacrifices when he got back to the temple (v. 9). Jonah had learned you cannot escape from God. He knew God had saved him from death. He was ready to tell that in temple worship.

God's mission was accomplished. He spoke to the fish, not to the prophet. The fish developed history's most horrible bellyache and vomited Jonah on land.

■ TRUTHS TO LIVE BY

The Sovereign God sends you where He will for His purposes. God does not call you to determine what you want to do and then to ask Him to bless your choice. Mission for God is not a smorgasbord of choices. It is a command to join God where He is at work. Will you?

The Sovereign God uses unexpected people and things to achieve His purpose. God wants to redeem the world. He wants to use you. When you rebel, He uses whom He can, even pagan sailors and dumb fish. Can He use you now?

The Sovereign God delivers you even when you rebel. Rebellion is not your last word to God. He does not accept it. He works again and again to woo you to Himself and to use you in mission. He forgives rebellion. Can you forgive yourself and let Him use you anew?

■ A VERSE TO REMEMBER

But Jonah rose up to flee unto Tarshish from the presence of the LORD.—*Jonah 1:3*

■ DAILY BIBLE READINGS

God Show Mercy

JONAH 3:1–4:11

Saying good-bye is hard. Sometimes we hate to say good-bye to the silliest things. Going to college, I said good-bye to baseball cards. Going to seminary, I said good-bye to Texas. Going to the foreign mission field, I said good-bye to a church I loved but also to a large part of my library. Returning from foreign fields, I waved to a mission dream and a fluffy white dog. Yes, I have said I love you and good-bye to many, often silly, things. Each time, I did it claiming I was following God's leading. God led Jonah to say good-bye several times and wanted him to say good-bye to some things He would not leave.

■ THE BIBLE LESSON

1 And the word of the Lord came unto Jonah the second time, saying,

2 Arise, go unto Nineveh, that great city, and preach unto it the preaching that I bid thee.

3 So Jonah arose, and went unto Nineveh, according to the word of the Lord. Now Nineveh was an exceeding great city of three days' journey.

4 And Jonah began to enter into the city a day's journey, and he cried, and said, Yet forty days, and Nineveh shall be overthrown.

5 So the people of Nineveh believed God, and proclaimed a fast, and put on sackcloth, from the greatest of them even to the least of them.

. . . .

10 And God saw their works, that they turned from their evil way; and God repented of the evil, that he had said that he would do unto them; and he did it not.

. . . .

1 But it displeased Jonah exceedingly, and he was very angry.

2 And he prayed unto the Lord, and said, I pray thee, O Lord, was not this my saying, when I was yet in my country? Therefore I fled before unto Tarshish: for I knew that thou art a gracious God, and merciful, slow to anger, and of great kindness, and repentest thee of the evil.

3 Therefore now, O Lord, take, I beseech thee, my life from me; for it is better for me to die than to live.

4 Then said the Lord, Doest thou well to be angry?

5 So Jonah went out of the city, and sat on the east side of the city, and there made him a booth, and sat under it in the shadow, till he might see what would become of the city.

. . . .

11 And should not I spare Nineveh, that great city, wherein are more than sixscore thousand persons that cannot discern between their right hand and their left hand; and also much cattle?

■ THE LESSON EXPLAINED

Good-bye to Home Missions (3:1–4)

One more try, Jonah. Nineveh is the destination I chose. Are you going?

Nineveh? Capital of Assyria. Most cruel nation on earth. Our biggest enemy. That strange language. So far away. I won't know anyone. You say You are going to judge and destroy them. Why tell them? They earned it. Go ahead and destroy. I'll tell people at home and let them see how great You are. I'll make sure You get the credit here.

I am working in Nineveh just now. I want you there.

On my way, Lord. Here I am in Nineveh, Lord. What a huge city, Lord. I was not prepared for this. I'll walk around a while. Then I'll preach. Okay, Lord, so I've been walking all day and said nothing. I'll preach. "Forty days and Nineveh destroyed." Good five-word sermon, huh, Lord? I preached. Time for You to destroy.

Good-bye to Judgment (3:5–10)

We heard Your word, Yahweh, God of Israel. We believe You mean what You say. Forgive us, Lord. Look, we are in mourning because of Your word. Everyone in town. The king has commanded mourning for all, even our animals. No one will eat a bite. We won't even take a sip of water. We have done wrong. We will do right. Can You forgive us, Lord Yahweh of Israel? Please.

What do you expect to happen? People repented. So did God. He changed His plans when they changed their ways. No judgment for Nineveh. No destruction.

Good-bye to Prejudiced Evangelism (4:1–11)

I knew it. God, I told you this would happen. You went back on Your word just as I said. That is why I did not want to come. Then You could have zapped Nineveh. But, no, You let them repent. You do not judge them. I am a fool. What I preached did not happen. What will people back home think? I know You are a God of love. But love has limits. You love the wrong people. You know, some people You are not supposed to love. I want a different kind of God. Just kill me if You are going to be that way.

Now, Jonah. Calm down. Are you really doing right to be so mad? Yes, I am. I am going to sit on this hill and wait for You to zap Nineveh. Here, Jonah. Sit under this nice vine I made for you. You will be cool in its shade. Thanks, Lord. That is wonderful.

Another surprise. Here is My little worm. He will eat the roots of the vine. Here's a hot east wind. Now, how do you feel, Jonah? Mad! Mad enough to die. Wait a minute. Does my prophet love a one-day gourd more than a mission? If you love the vine that much, can't I love Nineveh at least that much? Look at all the poor, innocent, ignorant people. Love them with Me. Or love your prejudice.

■ TRUTHS TO LIVE BY

God's world is bigger than yours. God calls you to a vision of mission where people have never heard. Are you content to do mission where everyone has at least heard?

God's love is bigger than His wrath. People want to pick and choose whom they love. We feel justified in anger against criminals, dirty people, uncultured people, foreign people, other races. A just God has the right to hate all of us and destroy us. He chooses to love. Will you?

God wants to cure your prejudice. You hate because you have learned prejudice against others. God loves because He is love. He can cure your prejudice and make you like Him. Will you let Him let you love?

■ A VERSE TO REMEMBER

I knew that thou art a gracious God, and merciful, slow to anger, and of great kindness, and repentest thee of the evil.—Jonah 4:2

■ DAILY BIBLE READINGS

Feb. 5 — Sin's Punishment. Gen. 19:25–29
Feb. 6 — Test of a True Prophet. Deut. 18:15–22
Feb. 7 — God Is in Charge. Lam. 3:31–39
Feb. 8 — Moral and Social Abuses. Mic. 1:1–10
Feb. 9 — Steadfast Compassion. Exod. 34:1–9
Feb. 10 — Recipe for Discouragement. 1 Kings 19:1–8
Feb. 11 — God's Logic. Jon. 4:6–10

The Loyalty of Ruth
RUTH 1

T ragic times. The seventies deserve that title in my family history in many ways. In a ten-year stretch death decimated us. Father-in-law, mother, mother-in-law, and finally father died. All the while an ocean separated us. Grief does not get properly served in a foreign country. Returning home somehow finds an empty hole never filled. Naomi discovered that in her ten-year trek to Moab. She discovered much more.

■ THE BIBLE LESSON

1 Now it came to pass in the days when the judges ruled, that there was a famine in the land. And a certain man of Beth-lehem-judah went to sojourn in the country of Moab, he, and his wife, and his two sons.

2 And the name of the man was Elimelech, and the name of his wife Naomi, and the name of his two sons Mahlon and Chilion, Ephrathites of Beth-lehem-judah And they came into the country of Moab, and continued there.

3 And Elimelech Naomi's husband died; and she was left, and her two sons.

4 And they took them wives of the women of Moab; the name of the one was Orpah, and the name of the other Ruth: and they dwelled there about ten years.

5 And Mahlon and Chilion died also both of them; and the woman was left of her two sons and her husband.

6 Then she arose with her daughters-in-law, that she might return from the country of Moab: for she had heard in the country of Moab how that the Lord had visited his people in giving them bread.

7 Wherefore she went forth out of the place where she was, and her two daughters-in-law with her; and they went on the way to return unto the land of Judah.

8 And Naomi said unto her two daughters-in-law, Go, return each to her mother's house: the Lord deal kindly with you, as ye have dealt with the dead, and with me.

. . . .

*16 And Ruth said, Intreat me not to leave thee, or to return from fol-
lowing after thee: for whither thou goest, I will go; and where thou
lodgest, I will lodge: thy people shall be my people, and thy God my God:*

*17 Where thou diest, will I die, and there will I be buried: the Lord do
so to me, and more also, if aught but death part thee and me.*

*18 When she saw that she was steadfastly minded to go with her, then
she left speaking unto her.*

■ THE LESSON EXPLAINED

Tragic Times (vv. 1–5)

I know I must face death and grief, but does it all have to come
at once? First, I lose my country because it supplies no food. Mov-
ing in with foreigners is not easy, especially when the only place to
go is a land our tradition calls enemy territory (see Deut. 23:3).
Then My children have to marry foreigners. My husband dies. My
sons die. Alone in enemy land with two foreign daughters-in-law.
How am I supposed to respond to such tragic times?

Testing Times (vv. 6–13)

Tragic times are testing times. They force new types of decisions when I feel least able to make any decisions. Tragedy in a foreign land brings even more tests. Stay? Return home? Depend on
what family is left? Give them their freedom and fend for myself?
Look for new relationships? Avoid as much chance of new tragedy
as possible? Try to make do on what little my husband left me?
Find ways to create new financial resources? All the decisions stare
me in the face. What do I do first?

Naomi passed that test easily. First, she had to find a place to
live. Moab certainly did not seem promising. The first bit of good
news in a long time offered a gleam of hope. God had lifted the
famine. Home produced food once more. I am going home.

One decision raised another test. What do I do with the girls? I
certainly cannot provide them husbands as the law of levirate marriage (Deut. 25:5–10) demands. Leave them here. Let them rejoin
their culture and not be plagued with the labels foreign bride, foreign widow, or couldn't find one of your own kind to marry. That

is the lonely way, but the only way. Now to tell the girls. Testing time becomes tearing time.

Trusting Times (vv. 14–18)

Good-bye, Orpah. I will never forget all you have meant to me and my family. Sorry things could not have worked out better. Surely the Lord will bless you in the years to come.

Now your turn, Ruth. Go back with Orpah. Find a good man. Settle down and have the good family you so richly deserve. You do not have to do anything else to show you love me. Now let loose of me and go back where you belong.

No, Mother Naomi. I will not go back. Do not ask me to leave you. Wherever you go, I go. I have no home but your home, no people but you and your people. Most of all, I have no God but your God. I am part of you, your people, and your traditions. I love you more than anyone else. I go with you to the grave. Until then, you are stuck with me. I love you! I trust you! I am yours!

Okay. Ready for the long trip. Let's go. Look at all the people waiting for us. It is good to be back home and know people remember you. Good to be where you feel trusted and wanted again. Nothing like family loyalty. But they must know something. I am not the same young Naomi they knew. God has dealt bitterly with me in these ten years. They cannot call me Naomi, meaning pleasantness. They must call me Mara, meaning bitterness. Now it's time for harvest. We must find work. Testing times continue even among the trusting times.

■ TRUTHS TO LIVE BY

Tragic times are coming. At some point in life each of us faces tragedy. That does not mean that God forgets us or punishes us for a time. It means we are human and face the time in life to meet death of family, change of residence, loss of resources, loss of jobs. Your love relationship or lack of it with God now determines how you will respond to tragedy then.

Tragic times bring testing times. Tragedy does not let you face it in quietude and rest. Tragedy brings emergency decisions to test you. Such decisions are God-sized ones. You need Him to help you make them. Is your relationship close enough that you can hear His voice?

Testing times try your loyalties. Tests tempt you to seek loneliness and turn bitter. They provide opportunity for you to show your loyalties and find who is loyal to you. Now is the time to build loyal relationships that will support you in tragic times of testing. Know whom you can trust now. You will have to know then.

■ A VERSE TO REMEMBER

Intreat me not to leave thee, or to return from following after thee: for whither thou goest, I will go; and where thou lodgest, I will lodge: thy people shall be my people, and thy God my God.—Ruth 1:16

■ DAILY BIBLE READINGS

Feb. 12 — A Forefather's Generosity. Gen. 50:15–26
Feb. 13 — Provision of Food. Exod. 16:9–21
Feb. 14 — God's Care for the Earth. Ps. 104:10–18
Feb. 15 — Bread for the Poor. Ps. 132:11–18
Feb. 16 — God's Faithfulness. Ps. 145:11–20
Feb. 17 — Loyal Commitment. 2 Tim. 2:3–7
Feb. 18 — Naomi's Considerate Behavior. Ruth 1:9–15

The Kindness of Boaz

RUTH 2-4

G od's call to kindness surely allows exceptions. Sometimes I need kindness shown to me. Just as when I face final oral examinations to allow me to write my dissertation at Vanderbilt. Of course, that is when my wife's grandmother calls. Just because she is over ninety years old and lives by herself. I have called time out on kindness this week. She cannot expect me to spend the night with her tonight. I must have my rest. "Be ye kind one to another, tenderhearted, forgiving one another, even as God for Christ's sake hath forgiven you" (Eph. 4:32).

■ THE BIBLE LESSON

1 And Naomi had a kinsman of her husband's, a mighty man of wealth, of the family of Elimelech; and his name was Boaz.

. . . .

8 Then said Boaz unto Ruth, Hearest thou not, my daughter? Go not to glean in another field, neither go from hence, but abide here fast by my maidens:

9 Let thine eyes be on the field that they do reap, and go thou after them: have I not charged the young men that they shall not touch thee? and when thou art athirst, go unto the vessels, and drink of that which the young men have drawn.

10 Then she fell on her face, and bowed herself to the ground, and said unto him, Why have I found grace in thine eyes, that thou shouldest take knowledge of me, seeing I am a stranger?

11 And Boaz answered and said unto her, It hath fully been showed me, all that thou hast done unto thy mother-in-law since the death of thine husband: and how thou hast left thy father and thy mother, and the land of thy nativity, and art come unto a people which thou knewest not heretofore.

12 The Lord recompense thy work, and a full reward be given thee of the Lord God of Israel, under whose wings thou art come to trust.

. . . .

13 So Boaz took Ruth, and she was his wife: and when he went in unto her, the Lord gave her conception, and she bare a son.

14 And the women said unto Naomi, Blessed be the Lord, which hath not left thee this day without a kinsman, that his name may be famous in Israel.

15 And he shall be unto thee a restorer of thy life, and a nourisher of thine old age: for thy daughter-in-law, which loveth thee, which is better to thee than seven sons, hath born him.

16 And Naomi took the child, and laid it in her bosom, and became nurse unto it.

17 And the women her neighbors gave it a name, saying, There is a son born to Naomi; and they called his name Obed: he is the father of Jesse, the father of David.

■ THE LESSON EXPLAINED

Kindness Discovered (2:1–23)

Testing, trusting times call for kind help. Ruth and Naomi found it in an unexpected place. Naomi carefully reviewed her family tree and found a man of wealth and prestige. At Ruth's request to help, she sent Ruth to him, to work, not to beg. She followed custom for the poor and gathered grain the reapers missed (see Lev. 19:9–10; Deut. 24:19–22). Ruth was more than a poor farmhand. She caught Boaz's eye. He quickly made provision to keep her near him and to protect her. Why? Boaz had his ear tuned to the gossip line. He knew all about her kindness to Naomi and her newfound loyalty to Israel. She became his special project. He provided for her needs. Naomi rejoiced in God.

Kindness Developed (3:1–18)

How far can you take a person's kindness? Naomi set out to see. She plotted her strategy. Party time could develop that kindness to its limits. How would Boaz react? Ruth dared to find out. He applauded her kindness in choosing him rather than a younger man (3:10). But Boaz had to stretch his kindness a bit further for things to work out. Someone else had first claim on Ruth to fulfill levirate law (Deut. 25:5–10).

Kindness and Destiny (4:1–22)

Kindness is not magic. It meets roadblocks. The next of kin proved interested (4:4), but only in the family land. A young woman goes with it? That is a bit much. No, thank you, I will pass. The roadblock quickly cleared, Boaz stepped in. Quickly, he settled legal details and then marital ones. God showed His kindness. A son was born. Bitter Naomi became blessed Naomi again. The grandson lay at her breast.

The story just begins there. The son became grandfather to David, the founder of Judah's royal dynasty and the beginning of God's messianic line. Kind Naomi, kind Ruth, and kind Boaz showed more than human kindness. They were instruments of God at work preparing to redeem the world. They let Him work His divine kindness through them.

■ TRUTHS TO LIVE BY

Kindness overcomes obstacles. Often kindness comes in our best days when all is going right. Ruth showed kindness amidst tragedy to Naomi. Boaz showed kindness amidst the busiest, most stressful business season of the year. Do you calendar kindness or react naturally in kindness?

Kindness creates ongoing action. Often kindness is a one-time tip of the hat to the less fortunate. Boaz shows that kindness looks after the welfare of another on an ongoing basis. Kindness does not show itself to people on your social level to get momentary praise. Kindness cares for another and seeks the best possible life for the other no matter what it costs you.

Kindness results in reward. Kindness does everything for nothing. Kindness is usually its own reward on earth. Being kind is a character trait that makes you feel good about yourself. God takes kindness a step further. He works through your kindness to reward people far beyond your dreams, for kindness is truly God's work. Ultimately, God works through your kindness to reach His purpose of world redemption. Boaz and Ruth's kindness led to the Messiah's birth. What can God do with your kindness?

■ A VERSE TO REMEMBER
Blessed be he of the LORD, who hath not left off his kindness to the living and to the dead.—Ruth 2:20

■ DAILY BIBLE READINGS
Feb. 19 — Gleaning the Field. Ruth 1:19–2:7
Feb. 20 — Befriended and Protected. Ruth 2:13–23
Feb. 21 — Aggressive Behavior. Ruth 3:1–13
Feb. 22 — Giving Encouragement. Ruth 3:14–18
Feb. 23 — Nearest Kinsman Declines. Ruth 4:1–6
Feb. 24 — Making a Formal Claim. Ruth 4:7–12
Feb. 25 — Blessed Descendants. Ps. 128:1–6

Parable of the Sower

MATTHEW 13:1-23

Jesus, the heart and soul of Christianity. The kingdom of God, the heart and soul of Jesus' teachings. Put the two together, and you have the exciting study opportunity we face together for the next five weeks. Put Jesus and God together and then Jesus and daily living together, and you have an exciting path to follow for three months. Do you share the excitement? You can only if you are experiencing God each day and seeking to find Jesus at work in your heart and in your world.

■ THE BIBLE LESSON

1 *The same day went Jesus out of the house, and sat by the seaside.*

2 *And great multitudes were gathered together unto him, so that he went into a ship, and sat; and the whole multitude stood on the shore.*

3 *And he spake many things unto them in parables, saying, Behold, a sower went forth to sow;*

4 *And when he sowed, some seeds fell by the wayside, and the fowls came and devoured them up:*

5 *Some fell upon stony places, where they had not much earth: and forthwith they sprung up, because they had no deepness of earth:*

6 *And when the sun was up, they were scorched; and because they had no root, they withered away.*

7 *And some fell among thorns; and the thorns sprung up, and choked them:*

8 *But other fell into good ground, and brought forth fruit, some an hundredfold, some sixtyfold, some thirtyfold.*

9 *Who hath ears to hear, let him hear.*

. . . .

18 *Hear ye therefore the parable of the sower.*

19 *When anyone heareth the word of the kingdom, and understandeth it not, then cometh the wicked one, and catcheth away that which was sown in his heart. This is he which received seed by the wayside.*

20 *But he that received the seed into stony places, the same is he that*

heareth the word, and anon with joy receiveth it;

21 *Yet hath he not root in himself, but endureth for a while: for when tribulation or persecution ariseth because of the word, by and by he is offended.*

22 *He also that received seed among the thorns is he that heareth the word; and the care of this world, and the deceitfulness of riches, choke the word, and he becometh unfruitful.*

23 *But he that received seed into the good ground is he that heareth the word, and understandeth it; which also beareth fruit, and bringeth forth, some an hundredfold, some sixty, some thirty.*

■ THE LESSON EXPLAINED

Parables: Jesus' Method (vv. 1–9)

Great distance separated Jesus from the people—the distance between heaven's kingdom and earth's security. How could He bridge the gap? Jesus chose the simple way, telling stories and inviting people to listen.

What busy adult would stop work to go listen to a peasant from the backwoods town of Nazareth tell stories? Almost everybody. He had to take a boat out into the lake so He could see the people and they could see Him.

He began His series of stories in simple fashion, turning their eyes to the farm fields to image a farmer sowing seed. As usual, the seed did not all succeed. Birds ate much of it. Hard rocks just below the surface forced some to sprout immediately with only shallow roots. The sun quickly disposed of them. Some seed fell where other seed—weed seed—had already staked out claim. The good seed offered no competition to the weed seed. Again, instant death.

What a sad story! Great toil and no results. Oh, but wait! Some seed fell on good ground. Worth all the hard work and wasted seed to see bountiful harvest from a small part of the seed sowed. And Jesus' conclusion to it all? Are you listening? Pay attention.

Kingdom Mysteries: the Purpose (vv. 10–17)

Jesus, what are You doing? Crowds followed Jesus. How could they understand His stories? Even the disciples could not! Patiently

Jesus let them in on kingdom mysteries. Not everyone can understand. That would make salvation too simple. Hear, understand,
and be part of the kingdom. Some would almost force all people
into the kingdom, even against . . . free will. God always allows you
the freedom to accept or reject Him. God in His sovereignty gets
His message through to those He gives spiritual insight. Note that
this passage goes no further than this; it does not explain to whom
God gives such insight, how He gives it, or why He does or does
not give it. It makes clear human responsibility to respond to God's
message and bear fruit while reserving to God the sovereignty to
determine how people enter the kingdom. Failure to respond
brings awesome consequences, loss of opportunity and possibility
to respond.

This is not a new method and a new path God has taken. He
called Isaiah to a similar task long before. Preach the kingdom, He
said, but know results will not please you (see Isa. 6).

God's kingdom blessings are yours. You experience in Jesus
and the kingdom He brings what all the Old Testament heroes had
longed for but never experienced. Parable preaching is a part of
God's plan. It prevents hard-hearted people from sharing in a kingdom designed for love-hearted people.

Fruitfulness: the Result (vv. 18–23)

The parable now becomes plain to those Jesus has given insight. Satan has many ways of deceiving people and taking away
the seed God sowed before it takes deep root in their hearts. The
seed may disappear immediately; that is, people may never give
consideration to the good news of the kingdom. It may appear to
grow a little; that is, people continue to listen, even join spiritual
activities, but never let the gospel message take root in their heart
and grow. It may be choked out by weeds; that is, people may seem
to be growing in the gospel for a good while, but the world's weeds
take control of the heart, and the gospel message disappears forever.

That means only one sign shows true conversion and faith. All
bear fruit. All live like Christ and reproduce with other Christians.
What a marvel that, with all the opposition, God's mysterious

gospel finds any ground that will bear fruit. What a miracle that such small seeds can produce such bountiful crops. That is kingdom work. That is God at work. Are you at work there too?

■ TRUTHS TO LIVE BY

Jesus' teaching attracts people. When Jesus is present in Bible teaching, people come. Done in human power, teaching may repel people. Done in God's power, it draws people to Him.

Disciples alone understand kingdom truth. Kingdom truth stands opposed to worldly truth. God's ways stand opposed to human ways. You must have a heart open to God's truth and opposed to worldly truth. Then you are His disciple.

Christ demands more than listening. Too often people are content to listen to Bible teachers and store away information. Too seldom do they let God change their hearts so they can understand kingdom teaching.

Deeds, not words, mark disciples. Disciples do not simply talk a good religion. Neither do they sit and compare results and growth with one another. Disciples find God at work in the kingdom and join Him in His labors.

■ A VERSE TO REMEMBER

But he that received seed into the good ground is he that heareth the word, and understandeth it; which also beareth fruit.—Matthew 13:23

■ DAILY BIBLE READINGS

Feb. 26 — Trouble with the Law. Matt. 12:1–8
Feb. 27 — A Day Separate from Others. Exod. 20:7–11
Feb. 28 — Regard for Human Need. 1 Sam. 21:1–6
Mar. 1 — Ripened Wickedness. Joel 3:13–20
Mar. 2 — Sowing Goodness. Gal. 6:1–10
Mar. 3 — Understanding and Faith. Matt. 13:10–17

Parable of the Unforgiving Servant
MATTHEW 18:21-35

The church remains active but in ruins. Why? Thirty years ago a woman began spreading gossip about a church leader. Both doggedly remained in the church fighting for leadership positions. Neither would face the other, listen to words from the other, or talk to the other. Most importantly, neither would forgive the other. Result: two angry women, one unhappy congregation, one dead church. Does the church still have hope? Jesus pointed the way.

■ THE BIBLE LESSON

21 Then came Peter to him, and said, Lord, how oft shall my brother sin against me, and I forgive him? till seven times?

22 Jesus saith unto him, I say not unto thee, Until seven times: but, Until seventy times seven.

23 Therefore is the kingdom of heaven likened unto a certain king, which would take account of his servants.

24 And when he had begun to reckon, one was brought unto him, which owed him ten thousand talents.

25 But forasmuch as he had not to pay, his lord commanded him to be sold, and his wife, and children, and all that he had, and payment to be made.

26 The servant therefore fell down, and worshiped him, saying, Lord, have patience with me, and I will pay thee all.

27 Then the lord of that servant was moved with compassion, and loosed him, and forgave him the debt.

28 But the same servant went out, and found one of his fellowservants, which owed him an hundred pence: and he laid hands on him, and took him by the throat, saying, Pay me that thou owest.

29 And his fellowservant fell down at his feet, and besought him, saying, Have patience with me, and I will pay thee all.

30 And he would not: but went and cast him into prison, till he should pay the debt.

31 So when his fellowservants saw what was done, they were very sorry, and came and told unto their lord all that was done.

32 Then his lord, after that he had called him, said unto him, O thou wicked servant, I forgave thee all that debt, because thou desiredst me:

33 Shouldest not thou also have had compassion on thy fellowservant, even as I had pity on thee?

34 And his lord was wroth, and delivered him to the tormentors, till he should pay all that was due unto him.

35 So likewise shall my heavenly Father do also unto you, if ye from your hearts forgive not every one his brother their trespasses.

■ THE LESSON EXPLAINED

The Problem: Limits on Forgiveness (vv. 21–22)

Master, You teach forgiveness. I want to obey You and get the blessings You promise. I want to be sure I understand exactly what You want. Tell me, when have I done enough of this forgiving to meet Your minimum requirements? When can I quit forgiving? That was Simon Peter's direct approach to Jesus. Jewish rabbis said forgive three times. Peter would be generous. He offered to forgive seven times. Jesus replied in His standard way: a parable. First, he silenced Peter with an unexpected requirement. Forgive until you lose count. Jesus refused to give minimum standards people could accomplish. He set no limits. Forgive always.

The Plot: Forgiven but Not Forgiving (vv. 23–31)

Jesus' story sounds all too familiar. Lord, I am sorry. Forgive me! I will never do it again. Don't make me sell everything I have. Surely you cannot want me to sell my wife and kids into slavery. Give me time. I will pay you. I know the debt is in the millions, more money than I have ever seen. I promise. I will pay it somehow.

Surprise. The master forgave the debt and kept the servant employed. No one had to be sold. Why? Because the master loved so much. For once a clear, easy to understand parable. Only God loves like that. Only God forgives like that. Jesus wants me to see how much I owe God and how much He loves and forgives me. Wait, the story continues.

The servant who owes so much knows the other side of the story. He has a position of authority. How else could he establish such a great debt? People owe him money. A new life, he thinks. I can live again. I need cash to operate. Where is the guy who owes me a hundred days' wages? He will never pay me if I do not force him to. Pay up, mister. Right now! Or you will get yours.

Patience! Patience! I will pay you soon.

Of course not! Justice must be served. To prison with you till you pay every last cent. The old fool forgave me, but I will never be so foolish.

You do not get away with that quite so easily. The one who owes you has friends. They know what your master did for you. They tell your master.

The Proclamation: Forgive or Face the Judge (vv. 32–35)

Jesus makes His point plain in this parable. No mystery. No guessing or wondering. You demanded compassion and forgiveness from God. To get it, you must let God's nature take charge of your heart. Forgive, even when it costs you money. Forgive until you lose count. Keep forgiving. You will face God someday, either as loving, forgiving Father or as angry, condemning Judge. It all depends on your heart: greed or forgiveness?

■ **TRUTHS TO LIVE BY**

To forgive is not human. We are selfish. We like to do the other person in so we can be on top. To follow your heart means doom for every other person. Forgiveness comes into play only when I need it.

To forgive is divine. God is love. That means He is slow to anger and loath to punish. His natural response is forgiveness, when you ask.

To forgive is to imitate God. The opportunity to forgive tests your discipleship. When love conquers greed, you know God controls your heart. You are His disciple.

■ A VERSE TO REMEMBER

Judge not, and ye shall not be judged: condemn not, and ye shall not be condemned: forgive, and ye shall be forgiven.—Luke 6:37

■ DAILY BIBLE READINGS

Mar. 4 — Warning Against Wrong Teaching. Matt. 16:5–12
Mar. 5 — Declaring One's Belief. Matt. 16:13–20
Mar. 6 — Sharing a Vision. Matt. 17:1–13
Mar. 7 — Healing a Child. Matt. 17:14–21
Mar. 8 — Paying the Tax. Matt. 17:22–27
Mar. 9 — Determining Greatness. Matt. 18:1–14
Mar. 10 — Handling a Grievance. Matt. 18:15–20

Parable of the Vineyard Workers

MATTHEW 19:27-20:16

A strange job for an eleven year old: running the payroll machine for the entire corporation. It taught me a lesson. I promised Dad I would work for nothing. He said he would give me a quarter an hour to make out payroll and post accounts receivable. I agreed. Then I saw how much everyone else made. I wanted a new deal. Dad said, Son, you have to learn to keep the deals you make. Funny, his Master taught something similar.

■ THE BIBLE LESSON

1 For the kingdom of heaven is like unto a man that is an householder, which went out early in the morning to hire laborers into his vineyard.

2 And when he had agreed with the laborers for a penny a day, he sent them into his vineyard.

3 And he went out about the third hour, and saw others standing idle in the marketplace,

4 And said unto them; Go ye also into the vineyard, and whatsoever is right I will give you. And they went their way.

5 Again he went out about the sixth and ninth hour, and did likewise.

6 And about the eleventh hour he went out, and found others standing idle, and saith unto them, Why stand ye here all the day idle?

7 They say unto him, Because no man hath hired us. He saith unto them, Go ye also into the vineyard; and whatsoever is right, that shall ye receive.

8 So when even was come, the lord of the vineyard saith unto his steward, Call the laborers, and give them their hire, beginning from the last unto the first.

9 And when they came that were hired about the eleventh hour, they received every man a penny.

10 But when the first came, they supposed that they should have received more; and they likewise received every man a penny.

11 And when they had received it, they murmured against the goodman of the house,

12 Saying, These last have wrought but one hour, and thou hast made them equal unto us, which have borne the burden and heat of the day.

13 But he answered one of them, and said, Friend, I do thee no wrong: didst not thou agree with me for a penny?

14 Take that thine is, and go thy way: I will give unto this last, even as unto thee.

15 Is it not lawful for me to do what I will with mine own? Is thine eye evil, because I am good?

16 So the last shall be first, and the first last: for many be called, but few chosen.

■ THE LESSON EXPLAINED

God Has Work for Everyone (20: 1–7)

Desperation drove people to the marketplace. They had to find someone with a day's work to offer. They needed to buy the day's bread for their family. No job; no denarius; a hungry family. Some came early. Others waited a while. Everyone without a job came.

The owner of the vineyard needed workers. Grapes had to be harvested now. He hired everyone he could find and told them to trust him. He would pay what is right. They needed bread. They went to work.

Jesus said the kingdom is like this. God has a harvest. He has a place for all to work in the harvest. You can trust Him. His pay scale is fair.

People Do Not Understand God's Pay Scale (20: 8–12)

Hiring time you are grateful for a job. At quitting time you want your money. You compare yourself to everyone else. They just worked an hour or two. I worked all day. They are getting one coin. What a gracious boss. I hope he hires me tomorrow. No one pays that much for a couple hours work.

What! I only get one coin? What happened to the gracious boss? He is not fair. I deserve more! How can I protest? Where is the judge? I will take him to court for unfair labor practices.

The Good God Does Not Bow to Human Standards (20: 13–16)
As long as you complain, you do not understand God, says Jesus. He does not follow human standards. He is the standard of goodness and justice. He gives you everything He promised you. You have no reason to expect more. He made a fair deal with you. You agreed. You kept your part of the bargain. He does, too. That is your personal relationship with God. Enjoy that relationship. Give God thanks that He allows you to join Him in His work and have a love relationship with Him. Do not compare yourself with other people. Do not envy the relationships God has with them or the rewards they seem to get. Trust God to be fair with them just as He always is with you. God's grace is never a reason for you to be angry. When you see God show love, rejoice. "The reason we object to equal treatment for all is precisely the objection of the workers in this parable—it doesn't seem fair. But we are fools if we appeal to God for justice rather than grace, for in that case we'd all be damned" (Craig L. Blomberg, "Matthew," *New American Commentary* 22, [Nashville: Broadman & Holman, 1992],304–05).

■ TRUTHS TO LIVE BY

God depends on people to accomplish His work. God's eternal plan puts the work of His mission in your hands. He says, go into all the world. Are you on the go for Him?

God determines the rewards you receive. You can trust His grace and fairness much more than any system you would contrive. Be grateful for His grace to you and for His grace to every other person, even when another seems to receive more grace.

God can reject those who think they are elect. Election is all in God's hands. It never gives you the right to make demands on Him. God never owes you anything. He has chosen to make salvation available, but He defines salvation. You are always working for Him. That shows you are elect in His grace.

■ A VERSE TO REMEMBER

So the last shall be first, and the first last: for many be called, but few chosen.—Matthew 20:16

■ DAILY BIBLE READINGS

Mar. 11 — God's Concern for the Poor. Deut. 24:10–15
Mar. 12 — A Disappointing Harvest. Isa. 5:1–7
Mar. 13 — God's Right to Choose. Rom. 9:14–24
Mar. 14 — A Day Fixed for Judgement. Acts 17:24–34
Mar. 15 — A Way to Behave. Lev. 19:9–14
Mar. 16 — A Sad Decision. Matt. 19:16–26
Mar. 17 — A Change of Mind. Matt. 21:28–32

The Parable of the Three Servants

MATTHEW 25:14-30

He had all the skill—personality, leadership, musical talent, public speaking ability. He had everything a young man could want. He used it hard and well. Money, family, travel, and recognition came his way. But then, family disintegrated, and greed for money replaced values Christian parents had so painfully instilled. Gradually, alcohol and sex dominated his life. The church never saw him again. Abilities found no outlet for use. The potential of youth dissolved into a middle-aged man's lost dreams.

■ THE BIBLE LESSON

14 For the kingdom of heaven is as a man traveling into a far country, who called his own servants, and delivered unto them his goods.

15 And unto one he gave five talents, to another two, and to another one; to every man according to his several ability; and straightway took his journey.

16 Then he that had received the five talents went and traded with the same, and made them other five talents.

17 And likewise he that had received two, he also gained other two.

18 But he that had received one went and digged in the earth, and hid his lord's money.

19 After a long time the lord of those servants cometh, and reckoneth with them.

20 And so he that had received five talents came and brought other five talents, saying, Lord, thou deliveredst unto me five talents: behold, I have gained beside them five talents more.

21 His lord said unto him, Well done, thou good and faithful servant: thou hast been faithful over a few things, I will make thee ruler over many things: enter thou into the joy of thy lord.

22 He also that had received two talents came and said, Lord, thou de-

liveredst unto me two talents: behold, I have gained two other talents beside them.

23 His lord said unto him, Well done, good and faithful servant; thou hast been faithful over a few things, I will make thee ruler over many things: enter thou into the joy of thy lord.

24 Then he which had received the one talent came and said, Lord, I knew thee that thou art an hard man, reaping where thou hast not sown, and gathering where thou hast not strewed:

25 And I was afraid, and went and hid thy talent in the earth: lo, there thou hast that is thine.

26 His lord answered and said unto him, Thou wicked and slothful servant, thou knewest that I reap where I sowed not, and gather where I have not strewed:

27 Thou oughtest therefore to have put my money to the exchangers, and then at my coming I should have received mine own with usury.

28 Take therefore the talent from him, and give it unto him which hath ten talents.

29 For unto everyone that hath shall be given, and he shall have abundance: but from him that hath not shall be taken away even that which he hath.

30 And cast ye the unprofitable servant into outer darkness: there shall be weeping and gnashing of teeth.

■ THE LESSON EXPLAINED

The Gift: God's Resources (vv. 14–15)

The kingdom of God is a travel narrative. The king plans an extended foreign journey and turns over responsibility of the kingdom to servants. The king knows the capabilities of each servant and divides responsibilities and resources accordingly. Every one gets something: one talent represented sixty days work for the average laborer. Each is expected to produce returns.

The Gain: Double or Nothing (vv. 16–18)

How do you view the kingdom? It is the most precious item in existence. I will do anything I can to help the kingdom. I will risk all I have. So said each of the two servants as they traded the king's resources until they had doubled their money. Oh, the kingdom is so precious. I will guard it with my life. I must defend the kingdom against all comers. So I will hide its resources so no one else can get to them. So said the third servant as he dug a hole and hid the kingdom resources away from everyone else's grasp. That's the two reactions to the kingdom. Risk everything for it, or try to protect it while risking nothing.

For the Good: Increased Responsibility (vv. 19–23)

The kingdom seems never to end, the king always away, never to return. But the day is coming when the king will return and distribute kingdom rewards. The greatest reward is joy. This comes by accepting the king's gift of increased responsibility, increased opportunity for risk taking. It matters not how much you received. The question is, did you value the kingdom, take the risk, and make the profit?

For the Guilty: Eternal Judgment (vv. 24–30)

The servant who plays life safe and sure came, expecting reward, too. He carefully laid out his plan of action and the reasons for it. He painted the worst possible picture of the king to justify his actions. The king's actions with the other servants shows He did not fit the third servant's description. Even if he had, that is no reason to act as the third servant did. He feared the king and did not want to disappoint him. He presented the king with just what the king had owned all along. Nothing risked. Nothing gained.

I had other plans, explained the king. I expected you to go where they charge high interest rates. Let them use my money and get the profit for me. I gave you a lot of opportunity. You wasted it. Now the chance is gone. Away with you. Eternal punishment. Not fair for a man who was simply careful and prudent. Totally fair, says God. I am not looking for people who play it safe. I am looking for people who risk it all to reach the highest kingdom potential.

■ TRUTHS TO LIVE BY

God provides resources for all His servants. God leaves no one without ways to serve His kingdom. Will you risk the abilities and possessions He gives you for kingdom business or worldly cares?

God expects returns from all. Timidity, fear, uncertainty, focus on God's wrath . . . nothing excuses you from taking risks to make God's kingdom grow. Kingdom work is fruit-bearing work.

God rewards risk. The Father knows your potential and so sets His expectations of you. He expects you to know your resources and how to invest them in kingdom-growing enterprises. Playing it safe is not the way of the kingdom. Risking all for Christ is.

God rejects hesitation and fear to act. The kingdom calls you to action. It leaves no room for spectators.

■ A VERSE TO REMEMBER

For unto everyone that hath shall be given, and he shall have abundance: but from him that hath not shall be taken away even that which he hath.—Matthew 25:29

■ DAILY BIBLE READINGS

Mar. 18 — Greatest Commandments. Matt. 22:34–40
Mar. 19 — Greatness Seen in Serving. Matt. 23:1–12
Mar. 20 — Hypocrisy Condemned. Matt. 23:13–26
Mar. 21 — The Pain of Rejection. Matt. 23:29–39
Mar. 22 — Unpredictable Event. Matt. 24:36–44
Mar. 23 — Punishment for Unfaithfulness. Matt. 24:45–51
Mar. 24 — Poor Preparation. Matt. 25:1–13

The Parable of the Great Feast

LUKE 14:1-24

What is God's kingdom like? It is Na'em, my college friend and fellow minister. He is an Arab. He lives on land Jews claim. He preaches Christ to all who will listen. His dark skin, Arabic accent, and Jewish homeland isolate him from most people by the world's standards. Christ's standards make him friend to all.

■ THE BIBLE LESSON

15 And when one of them that sat at meat with him heard these things, he said unto him, Blessed is he that shall eat bread in the kingdom of God.

16 Then said he unto him, A certain man made a great supper, and bade many:

17 And sent his servant at supper time to say to them that were bidden, Come; for all things are now ready.

18 And they all with one consent began to make excuse. The first said unto him, I have bought a piece of ground, and I must needs go and see it: I pray thee have me excused.

19 And another said, I have bought five yoke of oxen, and I go to prove them: I pray thee have me excused.

20 And another said, I have married a wife, and therefore I cannot come.

21 So that servant came, and showed his lord these things. Then the master of the house being angry said to his servant, Go out quickly into the streets and lanes of the city, and bring in hither the poor, and the maimed, and the halt, and the blind.

22 And the servant said, Lord, it is done as thou hast commanded, and yet there is room.

23 And the lord said unto the servant, Go out into the highways and hedges, and compel them to come in, that my house may be filled.

24 For I say unto you, That none of those men which were bidden shall taste of my supper.

■ THE LESSON EXPLAINED

The Context: Religion or Righteousness (vv. 1–6)

What do you do after worship? Lunch with friends? That was Jesus' way. One problem, though, was that His enemies came, too. (Compare 6:7; 11:53–54). They kept a close eye on Jesus. Other eyes watched. The sick sought opportunities for healing. Jesus watched for the Pharisees' reaction. Did their rules allow Him to help a sick person on the holy day? They watched their own reputation and said nothing to let Jesus embarrass them. So Jesus healed and questioned again. Would they help desperate animals on God's day? They refused His trap. Silence reigned, but a loud silence. Religion sought reason to rebuke. Righteousness found ways to revive.

The Cause: High Position or Humble Piety (vv. 7–11)

Silence was seldom Jesus' way. He told stories. A wedding feast made one point clear. Fame is given, not taken. Humility is God's way. It may lead to opportunity for recognition. Self-sought recognition flashes by and fades, for soon another deserves more recognition.

The Company: Nice or Needy (vv. 12–14)

Look who's coming to dinner! Jesus said, Expect the homeless and hungry. Seek them out and bring them in. What? Let them dirty up my house? Let the neighbors see such trash entering our nice neighborhood? Why would I do that? Simple. You belong to God's kingdom and put it first. Pleasing God is more important than pleasing neighbors, and God loves those we call unlovely. We like to be with the nice people. He seeks out the needy. He says, Follow me! Heaven beckons when you do.

The Conclusion: Alibi or Abide (vv. 15–24)

Finally, someone says something. A nice proverb should please Jesus. Jesus saw through the reasoning. Eating in the kingdom depends on how you eat here. Kingdom eating is like a great feast. The host invites guests who agree to come. The host prepares everything and sends a second invitation saying, now it's time to come. Accepting the first invitation is easy; you just make a promise with your lips. Living up to the promise when the time comes is more difficult. Too many things compete for your time. Most such excuses are lame, showing devotion to work and money rather than to friendship and festivity. How would you react to such excuses if you had prepared the feast for friends? God reacts the same way: angry at unfaithful people. God goes further: He sends to the streets. He will celebrate. He will have people in His kingdom, just not the ones expected. The kingdom comes. You may not, if you do not accept the invitation God gives now.

■ TRUTHS TO LIVE BY

God's kingdom surprises you. Those you look for do not come. They refuse to associate with the people God loves. Those you refuse to associate with find home and food in God's kingdom.

God's kingdom serves no one's pride. If you demand front row seats, forget it. God honors according to His plan and will. Humbly sit at the back and wait.

God's kingdom has no acceptable alibis. God is sovereign. He takes first place or no place in your life. When something becomes more important than God's invitation, something has replaced Him as your god. Kingdom reservations go to others.

■ A VERSE TO REMEMBER

And the LORD said unto the servant, Go out into the highways and hedges, and compel them to come in, that my house may be filled.—Luke 14:23

■ DAILY BIBLE READINGS

Mar. 25 — Always Prepared. Luke 12:35–40
Mar. 26 — Satisfaction in Obedience. Luke 12:41–48
Mar. 27 — Produce or Die. Luke 13:1–9
Mar. 28 — Misplaced Emphasis. Luke 13:10–17
Mar. 29 — Lost Identity. Luke 13:22–30
Mar. 30 — Determining Priority. Luke 14:1–6
Mar. 31 — Humility Honored. Luke 14:7–14

The Living Lord
LUKE 24:1–36

What is God like? That all-important question occupies us the next four weeks. More of the same, you say. Heard this all my life. Maybe so, but has head knowledge become heart knowledge? Is God more than an idea in your mind? Have you come to know Him well enough to say He is Lord, He is living, He shepherds my life, He is the vine providing nourishment each moment I live?

■ THE BIBLE LESSON

13 And, behold, two of them went that same day to a village called Emmaus, which was from Jerusalem about threescore furlongs.

14 And they talked together of all these things which had happened.

15 And it came to pass, that, while they communed together and reasoned, Jesus himself drew near, and went with them.

16 But their eyes were held that they should not know him.

17 And he said unto them, What manner of communications are these that ye have one to another, as ye walk, and are sad?

18 And the one of them, whose name was Cleopas, answering said unto him, Art thou only a stranger in Jerusalem, and hast not known the things which are come to pass there in these days?

19 And he said unto them, What things? And they said unto him, Concerning Jesus of Nazareth, which was a prophet mighty in deed and word before God and all the people:

20 And how the chief priests and our rulers delivered him to be condemned to death, and have crucified him.

21 But we trusted that it had been he which should have redeemed Israel: and beside all this, today is the third day since these things were done.

22 Yea, and certain women also of our company made us astonished, which were early at the sepulchre;

23 And when they found not his body, they came, saying, that they had also seen a vision of angels, which said that he was alive.

24 And certain of them which were with us went to the sepulcher, and found it even so as the women had said: but him they saw not.

25 Then he said unto them, O fools, and slow of heart to believe all that the prophets have spoken:

26 Ought not Christ to have suffered these things, and to enter into his glory?

27 And beginning at Moses and all the prophets, he expounded unto them in all the scriptures the things concerning himself.

■ THE LESSON EXPLAINED
Eyes That Cannot See (vv. 13–16)

Down the winding road walks a man. His garb, gait, and goal distinguish him from no one. Come, walk with us, two men on the road say. The time will pass faster in company. You have heard the latest rumors about that Jesus that so many thought was God's hope for Israel? At least, until Rome ended such hopes by hanging Him on the cross. Some women came claiming His tomb is empty. They say God raised Jesus from the dead! Can you believe such talk? For once, Jesus walked in silence, listening. The men walked on gabbing, blindly. God's moment of revelation had not come (see 9:45; 18:34).

Hearts That Do Not Believe (vv. 17–26)

Finally, Jesus spoke, What are you talking about? Why does it make you so sad? What is wrong with you? Everyone knows! How could you be so ignorant? The men replied, High hopes are dashed. Our Messiah is dead. Our own preachers turned Him in to the authorities. The Romans killed Him. Women claim they saw angels who said He is alive. Can you believe that?

Sure I can believe it, Jesus responded. Look at Scripture. Psalm 22 and Isaiah 53 pointed to this. Did you not listen to God's Word? Only fools refuse to believe. What are you?

Silent Symbols That Speak (vv. 27–35)

Now they were the silent ones. He spoke. As so often, He explained Scripture. Now they listened closely. Still, no understanding. He started to leave. Oh, no! You must spend the night with us. Again, He sat at a meal with friends. He did just what He did at the last supper before He gave Himself to die. Words had prepared the way. Symbols opened blind eyes and unbelieving hearts. This was Jesus. He is alive! How could we be so stupid? Jesus, Jesus, we have so many questions to ask you now. Where is He? He vanished. Oh, how our hearts burned as He talked. Now we know why. Everyone must hear about this. Forget about going to bed. Let's go back to Jerusalem and tell the disciples. Jesus rose from the dead. He is alive. The Lord lives. Hallelujah!

■ TRUTHS TO LIVE BY

The Lord lives, but you may not know Him. Jesus is alive. Stubborn, blind disciples finally became convinced. You may talk about this as fact. Only daily life shows if you truly know the living Lord.

The Lord lives, but you may not believe Him. God has done everything He can to introduce you to the living Savior. Scripture, family, friends, church, the Holy Spirit all tell you He lives. Still, in your heart lurks that awesome doubt. Is this more than a story with a happy ending? Does it make a difference for me?

The Lord lives and wants a love relationship with you. God wants you to know more than a story about Jesus. He wants you to know and love the risen Lord as your best friend. God loves you. He proved it on the cross. Give Him your love in return. Obey and experience Him as living Lord.

The Lord lives; tell everybody. The living Lord makes you restless. You cannot stick to the same routine. You must do something about the living Lord. You must tell your neighbor, your boss, your colleague, the homeless, the hungry, the weary, the poor, the wealthy. Tell everybody!

■ A VERSE TO REMEMBER

And beginning at Moses and all the prophets, he expounded unto them in all the scriptures the things concerning himself.—Luke 24:27

■ DAILY BIBLE READINGS

Apr. 1 — Before Pilate and Herod. Luke 23:1–12
Apr. 2 — Sentenced to Death. Luke 23:13–25
Apr. 3 — Nailed to the Cross. Luke 23:26–38
Apr. 4 — Wonderful Promise. Luke 23:39–43
Apr. 5 — Death of a "Good Man." Luke 23:44–49
Apr. 6 — Buried. Luke 23:50–56
Apr. 7 — Hard to Believe. Luke 24:1–12

The Loving God
LUKE 15:1-10

Barney was strange. Everyone agreed. Everyone except the young people down at the black mission. While we enjoyed the thrills and spills of normal college life, strange Barney spent his spare time at the mission—teaching, giving, sharing his life to make theirs better. Skin color, economic level, chance to gain something from time invested—such factors never entered Barney's mind. Why? God's love filled Barney's heart. I came to know God was love because I saw Barney give that love to the youngsters in the mission. I came to know God's love because I saw the youngsters find that love and give it back to Barney.

■ THE BIBLE LESSON

1 Then drew near unto him all the publicans and sinners for to hear him.

2 And the Pharisees and scribes murmured, saying, This man receiveth sinners, and eateth with them.

3 And he spake this parable unto them, saying,

4 What man of you, having an hundred sheep, if he lose one of them, doth not leave the ninety and nine in the wilderness, and go after that which is lost, until he find it?

5 And when he hath found it, he layeth it on his shoulders, rejoicing.

6 And when he cometh home, he calleth together his friends and neighbors, saying unto them, Rejoice with me; for I have found my sheep which was lost.

7 I say unto you, that likewise joy shall be in heaven over one sinner that repenteth, more than over ninety and nine just persons, which need no repentance.

8 Either what woman having ten pieces of silver, if she lose one piece, doth not light a candle, and sweep the house, and seek diligently till she find it?

9 And when she hath found it, she calleth her friends and her neighbors together, saying, Rejoice with me; for I have found the piece which I had lost.

10 Likewise, I say unto you, there is joy in the presence of the angels of God over one sinner that repenteth.

■ THE LESSON EXPLAINED

God's People Do Not Always Share His Love (vv. 1–3)

The wrong crowd. Pharisees always found Jesus there. Why? They separated the world into two groups: us and them, God's chosen and God's rejected. Jesus divided the world differently: people who needed God's love and people who did not think they needed it. He thrived among the first group and strived with the second.

Lost Property or Lost People (vv. 4–7)

The power and wonder of God's love! Jesus wanted everyone to share it. So He told stories about it. A shepherd has charge of one hundred sheep. One strays. What do I do? Protect ninety-nine? Or search for one? Clearly, you search for the lost. Or maybe you have another way. Take an inventory. Figure out which sheep is lost. Decide how much you value that sheep. Is that sheep worth your time and energy? Do you really want to risk your life for that sheep? Is it the wrong size, wrong shape, wrong breeding, wrong temperament, wrong influence on the other sheep? Of course, that is no way to go. You lost a valuable sheep. You forget all else and search.

Then you find it. What next? Rejoice with friends and family. What about your world of people? Same principle. Seek the lost, and celebrate when they are saved? Or as the Pharisees said, judge the lost, and wait until they find the way to act as you do. Protect property. Reject people. Jesus said, If property is so important, how much more important are people? Go find them, wherever and whoever they are.

Found Goods and Found Sinners (vv. 8–10)

Still you don't get it? Jesus has another story for you. You have ten dollar bills. One slips away under the couch. Lost. What do you do? Move the furniture; bring out the broom; get on your hands and knees—anything to find the ten dollars. Again, everybody, rejoice with me. I found what I lost. What about God? What brings rejoicing to heaven? Finding what God cares about most, a lost sinner. Now what brings happiness, joy, and rejoicing for you? Finding money or finding people?

■ TRUTHS TO LIVE BY

God loves sinners. A simple statement, but hard to believe. How can God love anyone not exactly like me? The answer! His doesn't. He loves all people just like you, all of them—sinners like you. He knows only saved sinners and lost sinners. How do you see people? Which do you love?

God searches for sinners. God's love is active, not passive. He searches for new people to love. He wants a love relationship with every person who ever lives. Joy pervades heaven when God's love invades a sinner, who thus evades hell.

God rejoices when you repent. Got the picture? You are the sinner God loves. When you repent, joy floods God. When you repent, God's love possesses you. That love blinds you to differences that might separate people. That love drives you to share His love with sinners. How much joy will you bring to heaven?

■ A VERSE TO REMEMBER

Likewise, I say unto you there is joy in the presence of the angels of God over one sinner that repenteth.—Luke 15:10

■ DAILY BIBLE READINGS

Apr. 8 — The Power of One. Matt. 18:10–14
Apr. 9 — Now Returned. 1 Pet. 2:18–25
Apr. 10 — Sinners Called. Luke 5:27–32
Apr. 11 — Sought and Saved. Luke 19:1–10
Apr. 12 — Freely Restored. Luke 15:11–24
Apr. 13 — Petty Self-Righteousness. Luke 15:25–32
Apr. 14 — Contending Loyalties. Luke 16:1–13

The Good Shepherd
JOHN 10:1–30

Sheep mean little to me. I have seen very few in my life. Shepherds mean a lot. Many people have shepherded me through trying moments of life. Leon was one of the first. A hulking two-hundred-twenty-pound tackle on a high school football team in the days when two-hundred-twenty-pounds was huge, Leon showed interest in a one-hundred-sixteen-pound boy too small to try out for water boy. At church and school Leon taught me the ropes of life and helped me steer clear of the dangers lurking before a high school freshman. Leon was my shepherd in high school because he knew the true Shepherd.

■ THE BIBLE LESSON

1 Verily, verily, I say unto you, He that entereth not by the door into the sheepfold, but climbeth up some other way, the same is a thief and a robber.

2 But he that entereth in by the door is the shepherd of the sheep.

3 To him the porter openeth; and the sheep hear his voice: and he calleth his own sheep by name, and leadeth them out.

4 And when he putteth forth his own sheep, he goeth before them, and the sheep follow him: for they know his voice.

5 And a stranger will they not follow, but will flee from him: for they know not the voice of strangers.

6 This parable spake Jesus unto them: but they understood not what things they were which he spake unto them.

7 Then said Jesus unto them again, Verily, verily, I say unto you, I am the door of the sheep.

8 All that ever came before me are thieves and robbers: but the sheep did not hear them.

9 I am the door: by me if any man enter in, he shall be saved, and shall go in and out, and find pasture.

10 The thief cometh not, but for to steal, and to kill, and to destroy: I am come that they might have life, and that they might have it more

abundantly.

11　I am the good shepherd: the good shepherd giveth his life for the sheep.

12　But he that is an hireling, and not the shepherd, whose own the sheep are not, seeth the wolf coming, and leaveth the sheep, and fleeth: and the wolf catcheth them, and scattereth the sheep.

13　The hireling fleeth, because he is an hireling, and careth not for the sheep.

14　I am the good shepherd, and know my sheep, and am known of mine.

15　As the Father knoweth me, even so know I the Father: and I lay down my life for the sheep.

16　And other sheep I have, which are not of this fold: them also I must bring, and they shall hear my voice; and there shall be one fold, and one shepherd.

17　Therefore doth my Father love me, because I lay down my life, that I might take it again.

18　No man taketh it from me, but I lay it down of myself. I have power to lay it down, and I have power to take it again. This commandment have I received of my Father.

■ THE LESSON EXPLAINED

Life or Loot (vv. 1–6)

The game is tug of war. You are the rope. Two sides pull at you to bring you to their side. Whom do you want to win? The world sends thieves and robbers. They see you as loot to be stolen away and used for their purposes. God sees you as a lost sheep, needing His love, protection, and care. God sent Jesus as the Good Shepherd to care for you. Thieves sneak in or climb over to get to you. Jesus knows the Creator's way to you. The gatekeeper recognizes His voice and no one else's. Jesus comes to call you to follow Him out to the best grazing places, where all the resources you need for life stand ready. He calls. Those who belong to Him follow. His is not the only voice. Others call. Jesus' people flee. And you? Whose call do you answer?

Life or Death? (vv. 7–10)

The choice is yours. Two paths beckon. Both promise great kingdoms for you. The one points to wealth, fame, glory, and happiness. The other points to humility, hope, and heaven. Whose claim do you believe? Why? Jesus calls forth. He is the doorway to heaven. No one else is. You must follow Him and let Him admit you to the Father's house. Otherwise, surprises wait for you. The doorway to wealth and glory opens into a detour. There the guides quietly shove you into the slaughterhouse. The doorway to wealth proves to be the doorway to doom. Time will soon be up. Which choice do you make? Jesus and life, or the world and death?

Sacrifice or Scatter? (vv. 11–18)

Two doors point to two shepherds. Whom will you trust to care for you, feed you, protect you, and determine your final destiny? The first shepherd created nothing and owns nothing. The flock has no personal meaning for this shepherd, for the shepherd has risked nothing for the flock. The first hint of danger finds the first hunt for personal safety. Forget the flock. Flee for your life. So what if sheep die? What does it matter if the flock scatters all over the hillsides, never to be gathered again? First things first. Save the shepherd's life.

The second Shepherd is totally different. He is good. He cares and loves the sheep. He risks His own life. Indeed, He willingly sacrifices His life for the sheep. He dies so they may live. He knows each sheep individually and can tell you the characteristics of each one. Why? He comes from the heavenly Father. He is in an unending love relationship with the Father. He spreads the Father's love to you, His sheep. But can I really belong to His flock? Is there not a limit on the number He can tend? Oh, no. He looks for still other flocks to tend. He is the only Good Shepherd. He wants to bring as many as possible into His fold. Will you come? Will you obediently listen to the Shepherd's call, obey His voice, and experience love from One who died for you?

■ TRUTHS TO LIVE BY

The world is not what it seems. The world and its leaders promise much. You stand before open doors labeled opportunity, wealth, fame, happiness. Entrance soon proves the labels false. The world's doors dazzle for a moment and then doom for eternity.

The Good Shepherd is truly good. The Good Shepherd went to the cross to prove His love for you. He tells you straight the life He offers, obedience to a cross. He shows you the gain: a love relationship with Him now and for eternity. Is this the kind of good you want?

The Good Shepherd's claims come from the one eternal God. Jesus does not share the world's motivation. He listens to the heavenly Father and obeys. God's eternal love lies behind everything Jesus says. Will you listen to His voice and obey? He will lead you to experience God and thus know eternal life.

■ A VERSE TO REMEMBER

I am the good shepherd; the good shepherd giveth his life for the sheep.—John 10:11

■ DAILY BIBLE READINGS

Apr. 15 — Aimlessness Challenged. Mark 6:30–34
Apr. 16 — Granted Privileges. Heb. 10:19–25
Apr. 17 — God's Resurrecting Power. Heb. 13:17–21
Apr. 18 — Corrupt Leadership. Ezek. 22:23–31
Apr. 19 — God Knows His Own. 2 Tim. 2:14–19
Apr. 20 — Genuine Security. John 10:22–30
Apr. 21 — Authenticated by Works. John 10:31–42

The True Vine
JOHN 15:1-17

An expert I was. The razzle-dazzle kid, I could answer almost any baseball question you could ask. Amazed adults with my baseball wizardry. Then the day came. Play ball, called the ump. I was at bat. Fastball. Never saw it. Strike one. Curve ball. Three feet separated the ball and my bat. Strike two. Waste pitch far outside and low. Fearfully, I swung anyway. Soon I led the league. Most strikeouts by a batter. Lowest on base percentage. Lesson learned. Expertise comes on the field, not in the mind. Jesus tried to teach the same lesson about religion. It is not what you know but to whom you have a relationship.

■ THE BIBLE LESSON

1 I am the true vine, and my Father is the husbandman.

2 Every branch in me that beareth not fruit he taketh away: and every branch that beareth fruit, he purgeth it, that it may bring forth more fruit.

3 Now ye are clean through the word which I have spoken unto you.

4 Abide in me, and I in you. As the branch cannot bear fruit of itself, except it abide in the vine; no more can ye, except ye abide in me.

5 I am the vine, ye are the branches: He that abideth in me, and I in him, the same bringeth forth much fruit: for without me ye can do nothing.

6 If a man abide not in me, he is cast forth as a branch, and is withered; and men gather them, and cast them into the fire, and they are burned.

7 If ye abide in me, and my words abide in you, ye shall ask what ye will, and it shall be done unto you.

8 Herein is my Father glorified, that ye bear much fruit; so shall ye be my disciples.

9 As the Father hath loved me, so have I loved you: continue ye in my love.

10 If ye keep my commandments, ye shall abide in my love; even as I have kept my Father's commandments, and abide in his love.

11   These things have I spoken unto you, that my joy might remain in you, and that your joy might be full.

12   This is my commandment, That ye love one another, as I have loved you.

13   Greater love hath no man than this, that a man lay down his life for his friends.

14   Ye are my friends, if ye do whatsoever I command you.

15   Henceforth I call you not servants; for the servant knoweth not what his lord doeth: but I have called you friends; for all things that I have heard of my Father I have made known unto you.

16   Ye have not chosen me, but I have chosen you, and ordained you, that ye should go and bring forth fruit, and that your fruit should remain: that whatsoever ye shall ask of the Father in my name, he may give it you.

17   These things I command you, that ye love one another.

■ THE LESSON EXPLAINED

Pruned or Perish (vv. 1–6)

God has His eye on you. The living, loving Owner of the vineyard will not ignore you. Why? You are firmly attached to His beloved Son. The Son is the vine. You are a branch attached to Him. What good news. Nourishment, growth, health is assured. The perfect Vine provides what the branches need. Better news. God has great faith in you. He expects a life of bounty, much fruit for many years. Bad news. You do not always produce. Then what!

God has two choices. First, He prunes you. He cuts off everything from your life that prevents you from producing fruit. He does everything possible to make you fruitful. The worst news. Pruned branches may still produce no fruit. They perish. God sends them to the rubbish heap. God does not accept fruitless branches.

How can you be sure you are pruned and don't perish? God's Word makes you that way. Feed on it. Faithful life in Jesus assures it. Abide in Him. He, not the world, is your abiding place. Separated from Him, you are a branch lying on the road waiting to die. You can do nothing.

Pray and Obey (vv. 7–10)

Afraid? Think your life is fruitless? Fear that God is about to make you fuel for the garbage heap fire? Jesus has assurance for you. The tools lie at your fingertips. You have nothing to accomplish. You need no special personal power. Just depend on Jesus. Live in His power. Let Him provide the housing and all your needs. Then listen. Let His words show you the pathway of life. His words do not return to Him empty.

When you become the residence of God's Word, you will bear fruit. Not because you are accomplished, but because you are abiding in Him and letting His Word abide in you. What a result! You have the right to ask God anything. His Word in you and your home in Jesus assure that what you ask is in line with His Word and His ways. Thus, God will answer the prayer, and you will bear fruit. Then God gains glory, for He, not you, provided the resources and power. You gain assurance. You are His disciple. What more could you ask?

You as the home of God's Word means you obey His commandments. The Word acts itself out through your life. The love relationship with God is secure. No reason to fear.

Joy in Jesus (vv. 11–17)

Jesus has one goal for you: joy. Joy is the reigning emotion in Jesus' life. He calls you to bear fruit, to abide in Him, to become the home where His Word lives, to bring God glory, to keep His commandments, to receive the love the Father gave Him and remain in it. Why? This brings joy to Jesus and to you.

But how can I know all the commandments and be sure I am keeping each of them? Jesus makes it easy. He gives one command that includes all the rest. Love one another. But how do I know how to express love? Look to Jesus. See how He treats you. He treats you that way because He loves you. He gave one great example of love—the cross. As long as you love enough to die, you will know how to act toward another person.

Loving others shows you are friends with Jesus. As friends, you get special information. You do not have to second guess God.

Jesus shows you everything God has shown Him. You know God's ways. Thus, you know the ways of love. Jesus chose you as friends. He does not make bad choices. He will ensure that you bear fruit. Just stay close to Him, love Him, let His words be at home in you. But remember. You must choose. Love Jesus, or love the world. You can't have it both ways. When you love Jesus, the world hates you.

■ TRUTHS TO LIVE BY

Disciples bear fruit. You can always know if you are Jesus' disciple. Your life will look like His, full of joy, love, and obedience. Such fruit attracts others to Jesus. Such fruit draws hatred from the world.

Disciples share Jesus' joy. Anger, frustration, hopelessness and fear mark separation from Jesus. Jesus gives joy. Religion without joy is religion without Jesus.

Disciples show Jesus' love. God is love. He loves Jesus. Jesus showed that love on the cross and shares that love with all who make their home in Him. Hatred for others shows distance from Jesus. Jesus' friends share God's love for all the world, every person in it.

■ A VERSE TO REMEMBER

I am the vine, ye are the branches: He that abideth in me, and I in him, the same bringeth forth much fruit: for without me ye can do nothing.—John 15:5

■ DAILY BIBLE READINGS

Apr. 22 — Preparing for the End. John 13:1–11
Apr. 23 — Telling What Would Happen. John 13:12–26
Apr. 24 — New Commandment. John 13:27–38
Apr. 25 — No Separation. John 14:1–7
Apr. 26 — God Revealed Through Christ. John 14:8–14
Apr. 27 — Continuing Guidance. John 14:15–20
Apr. 28 — To Love Is to Obey. John 14:21–31

Teachings About Happiness
MATTHEW 5:1-12

Hundreds of miles separated us from loved ones as we celebrated our first wedding anniversary in Europe. Across the miles came a card bearing the image of the bluebird of happiness. The note said, "May the bluebird of happiness bring you joy on this happy occasion." Happiness washed away tears of loneliness. We knew again that parents loved us despite miles and an ocean of separation. God plans an even greater happiness for you. This first lesson in a series of four will use Christ's Sermon on the Mount to paint the path of happiness for you.

■ THE BIBLE LESSON

1 *And seeing the multitudes, he went up into a mountain: and when he was set, his disciples came unto him:*

2 *And he opened his mouth, and taught them, saying,*

3 *Blessed are the poor in spirit: for theirs is the kingdom of heaven.*

4 *Blessed are they that mourn: for they shall be comforted.*

5 *Blessed are the meek: for they shall inherit the earth.*

6 *Blessed are they which do hunger and thirst after righteousness: for they shall be filled.*

7 *Blessed are the merciful: for they shall obtain mercy.*

8 *Blessed are the pure in heart: for they shall see God.*

9 *Blessed are the peacemakers: for they shall be called the children of God.*

10 *Blessed are they which are persecuted for righteousness' sake: for theirs is the kingdom of heaven.*

11 *Blessed are ye, when men shall revile you, and persecute you, and shall say all manner of evil against you falsely, for my sake.*

12 *Rejoice, and be exceeding glad: for great is your reward in heaven: for so persecuted they the prophets which were before you.*

■ THE LESSON EXPLAINED

The Sermon's Setting: Preparing Disciples (vv. 1–2)

Who could possibly live as Jesus described? He demands the impossible! So we reason as we approach this majestic summary of Christ's ethical teachings that we call the Sermon on the Mount. The Bible refuses to let us ignore the sermon so easily. It says Jesus taught this because disciples became hungry for directions for living. Jesus' response to their hunger is the Sermon on the Mount, His basic expectations of disciples. He never claims we will truly fulfill the expectations, but He never gives us reason to expect less from ourselves.

Finding Earthly Happiness (vv. 3–7)

Do I want to be blessed? What am I getting with blessing? You are drawn into God's arena of salvation. You become part of creating the environment of joy and happiness and redemption that is God's purpose for the world He created. You are thus truly happy in a way that includes hope and help for other people, not just selfish concentration on personal affairs and attitudes.

What can give me this kind of happiness? Jesus painted a clear picture. Such happiness comes both in earthly situations and ultimately in heaven. Declaring spiritual bankruptcy is the doorway to kingdom membership. Until you realize you cannot earn or power your way into God's kingdom, you cannot enter. Admitting you need spiritual resources does not come as you die and approach heaven's gates. It comes on earth as you commit your life to God through Christ.

Mourning brings happiness? How? Mourning means grief. That is the dilemma of God's kingdom. Happiness comes only as you mourn your lack of spiritual resources. Often this comes only through mourning the lack of material and spiritual needs in a specific situation of life. Happiness comes as God leads you through grief to rest in His happiness.

Meekness sounds weak but proves to be strong. Such gentle humility admits the power of others and the weakness of self. God surprises such people. They join Him in ruling the world. They become God's model for His final kingdom rule.

Hunger and thirst surely does not picture happiness, only hurt and need. That is true unless the hunger is for God's righteous rule to establish the standards by which all people live, so no one suffers need and injustice.

Being merciful seems a way to happiness. I find joy in helping family and friends in need. But do you find happiness in showing the same spirit to all people you meet, especially those the world ignores and leaves in poverty, misery, and hopelessness? Only as God lives in you to show mercy do you experience God's grace and mercy of forgiveness.

Finding Heavenly Happiness (vv. 8–12)

Earthly happiness is based on God's intervention in your life as you establish a lifestyle of humility, mourning, meekness, thirst for His righteous standards, and being merciful. Such happiness quietly blends into heavenly happiness as God moves you from this world to the next and establishes you as part of His eternal kingdom.

Such happiness results in extraordinary experiences with God. You see God at work on earth and then face to face in heaven. You find identity as God's child and seek no other identity on earth or in heaven. You participate in His kingdom as important members, first on earth and finally in heaven. You gain the rewards of residence in heaven with God for eternity.

How does this transition come about? Simply, as God so controls your life that you make peace with all people rather than feuding and fighting. Your heart becomes pure like Christ's heart because Christ lives in you, changing all desires and motivation. You expect and accept persecution on earth, knowing it marks your lifestyle as Christ-like, not worldlike. You join the long line of witnesses who prefer God's form of happiness to the world's promises.

■ TRUTHS TO LIVE BY

Happiness comes as God's gift, not the world's reward. Only God can make you into the kind of person He wants to join Him in establishing His kingdom on earth as it is in heaven. As He makes you this kind of person, He gives you a serenity of mind and satisfaction of identity that comes only when you are God's child doing His will.

Happiness comes amid earthly sorrow. Mourning, grief, hunger, and ignoring persecution do not fit the world's recipe for happiness. They are God's ingredients, showing you have placed God first in life and ignored all the world claims.

Happiness accompanies you from earth to heaven. God's blessing and happiness always enter your life in this world amid life's frustrations and pains. Giving you the peace of mind to make peace in the midst of human warfare, such happiness transforms you into a kingdom citizen and finally goes with you in its fullness in heaven.

A VERSE TO REMEMBER

Rejoice, and be exceeding glad: for great is your reward in heaven.—Matthew 5:12

■ DAILY BIBLE READINGS

Apr. 29 — Acceptable Sacrifice. Ps. 51:10–17
Apr. 30 — Comfort for the Distressed. Isa. 61:1–6
May 1 — Support for the Meek. Ps. 37:8–13
May 2 — Confident of God's Help. Isa. 26:7–15
May 3 — God's Gracious Mercy. Ps. 103:6–14
May 4 — Necessity of Peace. Heb. 12:12–17
May 5 — Prayer for Deliverance. Ps. 7:1–8

Teaching About Loving Your Enemies

MATTHEW 5:38-48

preached against some things I thought he was doing wrong. He voted against my plans for the church. A donnybrook stood in the offing. With whom would the church take sides? Who would win the fights to come? Then the seasoned deacon came to the young pastor for a private talk. He described a way to go, admitting where he had been wrong and letting me confess my own faults. His love for the church and for his pastor opened the door to fruitful ministry because he slammed the door on hatred, distrust, and being enemies.

■ THE BIBLE LESSON

38 Ye have heard that it hath been said, An eye for an eye, and a tooth for a tooth:

39 But I say unto you, That ye resist not evil: but whosoever shall smite thee on thy right cheek, turn to him the other also.

40 And if any man will sue thee at the law, and take away thy coat, let him have thy cloak also.

41 And whosoever shall compel thee to go a mile, go with him twain.

42 Give to him that asketh thee, and from him that would borrow of thee turn not thou away.

43 Ye have heard that it hath been said, Thou shalt love thy neighbor, and hate thine enemy.

44 But I say unto you, Love your enemies, bless them that curse you, do good to them that hate you, and pray for them which despitefully use you, and persecute you;

45 That ye may be the children of your Father which is in heaven: for he maketh his sun to rise on the evil and on the good, and sendeth rain on the just and on the unjust.

46 For if ye love them which love you, what reward have ye? do not even the publicans the same?

47 And if ye salute your brethren only, what do ye more than others? do not even the publicans so?

48 Be ye therefore perfect, even as your Father which is in heaven is perfect.

■ THE LESSON EXPLAINED

Tradition Says: Revenge, Hate (vv. 38, 43)

Get him before he gets you. Guard your back side. Stand up and fight like a man. No one's going to do that to my brother and get away with it. On and on go the traditions we learned as a kid. Each teaches us to stand up for our own rights and fight back when someone threatens us. We can justify such teaching by quoting Bible verses: "If a man cause a blemish in his neighbor; as he hath done, so shall it be done to him; Breach for breach, eye for eye, tooth for tooth: as he hath caused a blemish in a man, so shall it be done to him again" (Lev. 24:19–20).

We forget a few things. The Old Testament was not prescribing what you had to do to get even. It sought to prevent you from doing too much, retaliating too harshly. An injured eye was all you could demand for an injured eye. You had no right to do more than what one did to you. We don't read tradition that way. We don't look for limits put on us. We look to see how much we can get away with, how we can express our anger.

Whom does God want me to hate? Whom will He allow me to hate? Everything in my upbringing teaches me hatred for criminals, the lazy, IRS agents, used car dealers. The list goes forever. Hatred is a part of life.

Christ Calls: Leave Alone and Love (vv. 39–42, 44)

Jesus shocked His audience. If you listen, you will be no less shocked. Jesus drew absolute lines without excuses. Love rules your conduct. Legally, you may have the right to hurt someone else, fight back, limit your losses, and go only so far in obeying authorities. You may condemn a lazy beggar. Jesus says, love as God loves you. Do you deserve what God gives? Then don't put other people to the test to see if they absolutely deserve your love and what they are taking from you or asking of you. To follow Jesus is to forget rules and rights. To follow Jesus is to look for the best way to help other people, show God's love, and make peace. God's ways shock the world. The world always knows a better way to get ahead. Jesus shows the better way to join the kingdom.

The Father's Purpose: Perfect Family (vv. 45–48)

Why follow God's shocking way? The world's way looks so sure and safe. Besides, I find hatred and revenge a part of my nature. I can't avoid it. Jesus asks, how do you identify yourself? Do you belong to the world or to God?

God's children have identifying marks. The easiest to spot is unselfish love. God provides for both the good people and the not so good people. So should you. Everybody loves people who love them. The world's worst even know that kind of love. God calls you to be different. No excuses. No second-rate, minimal standards and expectations of yourself. Love as He loves. Be perfect as He is perfect. Let Him live in and through you. Become a mirror of God to the world.

■ TRUTHS TO LIVE BY

Love guides God's people, not hatred. God is love and creates His love in our hearts as Jesus lives in us. Hatred means we follow other people, not Jesus.

Enemies of God's people have no one to fight. God's people refuse to fight back, so our enemies become frustrated in their desire for a fight. They see only love facing them.

Love, not rules, guides Christian living. God made people free, able to apply love in specific situations and free to ask for His guidance in facing tough situations. God did not give rules to obey and claim personal goodness.

God expects perfection, nothing less. A forgiving God still does not let us live life expecting forgiveness in advance. He calls us to expect perfection from ourselves, for we are in His image and have Christ in us.

■ A VERSE TO REMEMBER

But I say to you, Love your enemies, bless them that curse you, do good to them that hate you, and pray for them which despitefully use you, and persecute you.—Matthew 5:44

■ DAILY BIBLE READING

Teaching About Riches and Anxiety

MATTHEW 6:19-21,24-34

Back from the mission field. Twenty-five years schooling and ten years of mission service behind us. No pension benefits built up. Two boys to educate. Virtually no savings. Only an entry-level job. What would we do? That old demon worry threatened to take over our lives. God, however, proved stronger than demon worry. He directed in ways unexpected and undeserved. We learned that today's world will never offer financial peace and security. God's way always points to His peace and security.

■ THE BIBLE LESSON

19 *Lay not up for yourselves treasures upon earth, where moth and rust doth corrupt, and where thieves break through and steal:*

20 *But lay up for yourselves treasures in heaven, where neither moth nor rust doth corrupt, and where thieves do not break through nor steal:*

21 *For where your treasure is, there will your heart be also.*

. . . .

24 *No man can serve two masters: for either he will hate the one, and love the other; or else he will hold to the one, and despise the other. Ye cannot serve God and mammon.*

25 *Therefore I say unto you, Take no thought for your life, what ye shall eat, or what ye shall drink; nor yet for your body, what ye shall put on. Is not the life more than meat, and the body than raiment?*

26 *Behold the fowls of the air: for they sow not, neither do they reap, nor gather into barns; yet your heavenly Father feedeth them. Are ye not much better than they?*

27 *Which of you by taking thought can add one cubit unto his stature?*

28 *And why take ye thought for raiment? Consider the lilies of the field, how they grow; they toil not, neither do they spin:*

29 *And yet I say unto you, That even Solomon in all his glory was not*

arrayed like one of these.

30 *Wherefore, if God so clothe the grass of the field, which today is, and tomorrow is cast into the oven, shall he not much more clothe you, O ye of little faith?*

31 *Therefore take no thought, saying, What shall we eat? or, What shall we drink? or, Wherewithal shall we be clothed?*

32 *(For after all these things do the Gentiles seek:) for your heavenly Father knoweth that ye have need of all these things.*

33 *But seek ye first the kingdom of God, and his righteousness; and all these things shall be added unto you.*

34 *Take therefore no thought for the morrow: for the morrow shall take thought for the things of itself. Sufficient unto the day is the evil thereof.*

■ THE LESSON EXPLAINED

Your Occupation: For Here or for Him (vv. 19–21)

"We try so hard to create heaven on earth and to throw in Christianity when convenient as another small addition to the so-called good life" (Blomberg, "Matthew," *NAC* 22, 124). Our total concentration on work has added a new word to the dictionary: workaholic. Nine to five has become six to midnight. Work consumes our lives.

Why? We never get enough. We do not enjoy what we do get. What time we do not work we spend worrying we are going to lose what we have. We prove Jesus right again and again. Our heart is dedicated to working for treasure. "Jesus commands his followers not to accumulate possessions they do not use for his work" (Blomberg, 122).

Earthly treasures vanish. Heavenly treasures multiply throughout eternity. You know the choice you should make. Your time card shows what choice you do make. Where is your heart?

Your Operation: Creating Light or Darkness (vv. 22–24)

I've had my eye on that for a long time. One day soon I am going to get it. Yes, we operate life with our eyes on something we desperately want. But is the apple of our eye going to create good or evil, light or darkness for ourselves, our family, our church, our world? Sadly, too often we do not know the answer. We are confused. We assume what we want will be good. In reality, it makes us more selfish, wastes our time and resources, robs our family of our presence, takes us away from church, and leads to no good. Oh, no. Not me. I will continue serving God. This other thing I just have to have is only a sideline activity. Not so, says Jesus. Either I am your master, or this thing you have your eye on is your master. Which will control your life: what you want to buy or Me? Serving both is impossible. Make your choice. Create light or darkness. See God or material things you buy. Which will it be?

Your Objective: Worldly Wares or God's Kingdom (vv. 25–34)

I can't forget about material goods. I have to have them every day. Just getting by consumes all my energy. That's the real world we live in. Yes, I know, says Jesus. After all I was there in creation. I know where all material things come from. Take a minute. Look at the birds. Do they have to worry about food? Or the flowers? Do they have to sweat it out to see if they will have quality clothing? What do you really get from all your worrying? Even King Solomon, the richest of all people, could not clothe himself better than God clothes the flowers.

What do you think? Are flowers more important to God than you are? Did He make flowers in His image? You worry because you refuse to believe. Worry is not God's will. Scratch worry out of your life. Every time you worry you act like pagans serving gods they cannot trust. God knows what you need. You must choose an objective in life. Trust yourselves for material things. Or trust God.

Either way, God expects you to have a job and work. He gave you work as part of human life in the Garden of Eden. Working is not the problem. Making work the center of life, worrying about things, not trusting God to supply your needs and lead you in the path that is best for you and your family—this is the problem. Tend to today. Do the work God provides today. Use the resources He gives today. Let God take tomorrow in His hands. Remember this: "Most individual and church budgets need drastic realignment in terms of what Christians spend on themselves versus what they spend on others" (Blomberg, 126–27).

■ TRUTHS TO LIVE BY

God will supply your daily needs. When you let God determine what you need, you can trust Him to supply those needs, often in ways you do not expect.

God sees your work as a way to serve Him, not a means to worldly wealth and security. God gives you work as a means of continuing His plans for creation. He expects you to use your occupation to serve His kingdom purposes.

God sees worry as a waste of time and energy. God is your Father. He loves you. He promises to care for your needs. Worry destroys you and shows how little faith you have in the Father.

God supplies needs according to His timing. Worry normally deals with things we can do without or which we do not yet need. Worry frets over tomorrow. God supplies today.

■ A VERSE TO REMEMBER

But seek ye first the kingdom of God, and his righteousness; and all these things shall be added unto you.—Matthew 6:33

■ DAILY BIBLE READINGS

May 13 — Seeking God's Approval. Gal. 1:6–10
May 14 — Praising God for His Care. Ps. 147:1–11
May 15 — Human Life Is Short. Ps. 39:1–13
May 16 — A Queen's Appraisal. 1 Kings 10:1–7
May 17 — Confident of God's Watchcare. Ps. 23:1–6
May 18 — Rewarded for Liberality. Ps. 37:21–26
May 19 — Folly of Self-Centeredness. Luke 12:13–21

Teaching About Prayer

MATTHEW 6:5-15

My beloved mother-in-law lay sick unto death hundreds of miles across the ocean. I could do nothing to help. I finally learned to pray. I tried every kind of prayer: praise, lament, thanksgiving, petition. I looked every day to see how prayer was answered. I kept hoping for news of recovery. Such news never came, but we did get to return home on furlough. My wife got to be with her mother as she died. We continue to miss the love, prayer strength, and fun she brought to our lives. Yet in her death, she taught us more than in her life, for she got us in honest, daily touch with the Father, letting Him hear the true cries of our heart and letting us learn how the Father answers prayer when we cannot have what we want.

■ THE BIBLE LESSON

5 *And when thou prayest, thou shalt not be as the hypocrites are: for they love to pray standing in the synagogues and in the corners of the streets, that they may be seen of men. Verily I say unto you, They have their reward.*

6 *But thou, when thou prayest, enter into thy closet, and when thou hast shut thy door, pray to thy Father which is in secret; and thy Father which seeth in secret shall reward thee openly.*

7 *But when ye pray, use not vain repetitions, as the heathen do: for they think that they shall be heard for their much speaking.*

8 *Be not ye therefore like unto them: for your Father knoweth what things ye have need of, before ye ask him.*

9 *After this manner therefore pray ye: Our Father which art in heaven, Hallowed be thy name.*

10 *Thy kingdom come. Thy will be done in earth, as it is in heaven.*

11 *Give us this day our daily bread.*

12 *And forgive us our debts, as we forgive our debtors.*

13 And lead us not into temptation, but deliver us from evil: For thine is the kingdom, and the power, and the glory, forever. Amen.

14 For if ye forgive men their trespasses, your heavenly Father will also forgive you:

15 But if ye forgive not men their trespasses, neither will your Father forgive your trespasses.

■ THE LESSON EXPLAINED

How Not to Pray (vv. 5–8)

Prayer belongs to religion. Almost all people pray. Too few know how. Too many know the wrong ways to pray. What makes a good prayer anyway? The one done so the most people can hear it? Certainly not. That makes people, not God, the audience of prayer. God has no place reserved for prayer where you must go to be heard. God hears you from any place. Hide yourself as cleverly as possible from people. God will hear you.

What is good prayer? Long times, complex sentences, holy words, impressive tones? No. You do not have to get God's attention. He is always attentive to your prayer needs. He never sleeps or takes a vacation. Tell Him what you have to say quickly and clearly. Do not try to impress God or people. Try to impress on God the faith you have in Him and the intensity you feel as you come to Him for help or praise.

How to Pray (vv. 9–13)

Christ presented the basic elements and attitudes of prayer. To whom do you pray? To the one God, who lives in heaven independent of all things on earth. What is this God like? He is holy, totally different from sinful human beings and thus the only One qualified to help us. What is the purpose of prayer? To establish a relationship with God that leads to making His kingdom come on earth. That means setting God's will as the center of my life, letting Him rule me here as He rules heaven's inhabitants.

Does that mean I cannot ask God for something for myself? Certainly not. You ask for things that are part of His kingdom and help establish His will. He created you and wants to satisfy each of your daily needs. Ask Him to supply what you need today and to let you see how that is part of His will. Ask Him to forgive you so that guilt will not prevent you from forgiving others. Commit yourself to be forgiving as He is forgiving.

What about all the problems I face? Is God concerned about those? Of course. He simply sees your problems in a different light. He sees them as temptations to do your will and not His, to help the cause of evil and not of the Good. Ask God to help you face your problems in a way that will establish His kingdom forever rather than in ways that help the evil one in his nefarious work. Confess God's greatness, and commit yourself to let the world see that greatness. That is prayer.

The Accomplishments of Prayer (vv. 14–15)

I prayed. What did I accomplish? Did I change anything in the world? Jesus promises you one major accomplishment. You established your relationships correctly. Guilt no longer separated you from God or from other people. He forgave you. You forgave other people. Love can flow between you and God and between you and other people. This is the beginning of God's kingdom, for the God who is love has a kingdom of love. Unforgiven sin and guilt are the major barriers to the kingdom coming on earth as it is in heaven.

TRUTHS TO LIVE BY

Prayer is an attitude, not an oration. Too often we see prayer only in view of the few people who lead in public prayer and repeat the same words every week. We need to see prayer as our constant attitude of commitment to God's kingdom and His loving forgiveness.

Prayer is a relationship, not a recipe. Prayer often becomes a recipe showing us how to get what we want from God. Jesus shows us that prayer is a relationship of trust in which we tell God our needs, establish our trust in Him as the unique and holy Creator and Provider, and echo His forgiving love in our relationship with all other people.

Prayer is kingdom business, not earthly preoccupation. Prayer frequently deals only with our problems and our desires and earth's enigmas. Jesus' prayer centers on bringing God's kingdom to reality in our lives and then on all of God's creation. Prayer puts us in a position and an attitude to join God in His work of redeeming the earth.

A VERSE TO REMEMBER

But thou, when thou prayest, enter into thy closet, and when thou has shut thy door, pray to thy Father which is in secret; and thy Father which seeth in secret shall reward thee openly.
— Matthew 6:6

■ DAILY BIBLE READINGS

May 20 — God Understands. Jer. 17:5–11
May 21 — Restraint in Using Words. Eccles. 5:1–7
May 22 — God Cares for His Children. Deut. 32:4–8
May 23 — God's Holiness. Isa. 6:1–8
May 24 — Prayer for Others. Eph. 3:14–21
May 25 — Conditions for Answered Prayer. 2 Chron.7:14–22
May 26 — How to Pray. Luke 11:1–13

Faith and Faithfulness

JAMES 1:1-27

You come to know God by experience as you obey Him and He accomplishes His work through you." Henry Blackaby has taught this biblical truth to thousands of people across the world through his conferences, workbooks, and study Bible on experiencing God. (See *The Experiencing God Study Bible*, [Nashville: Broadman & Holman Publishers, 1994], vii). The Book of James will teach us the power of obedience during the next five weeks. Are you willing to learn about James's practical religion of faith and obedience? Are you ready to obey?

■ THE BIBLE LESSON

2 *My brethren, count it all joy when ye fall into divers temptations;*
3 *Knowing this, that the trying of your faith worketh patience.*
4 *But let patience have her perfect work, that ye may be perfect and entire, wanting nothing.*

. . . .

12 *Blessed is the man that endureth temptation: for when he is tried, he shall receive the crown of life, which the Lord hath promised to them that love him.*
13 *Let no man say when he is tempted, I am tempted of God: for God cannot be tempted with evil, neither tempteth he any man:*
14 *But every man is tempted, when he is drawn away of his own lust, and enticed.*
15 *Then when lust hath conceived, it bringeth forth sin: and sin, when it is finished, bringeth forth death.*

. . . .

19 *Wherefore, my beloved brethren, let every man be swift to hear, slow to speak, slow to wrath:*
20 *For the wrath of man worketh not the righteousness of God.*
21 *Wherefore lay apart all filthiness and superfluity of naughtiness, and receive with meekness the engrafted word, which is able to save your souls.*

22 But be ye doers of the word, and not hearers only, deceiving your own selves.

23 For if any be a hearer of the word, and not a doer, he is like unto a man beholding his natural face in a glass:

24 For he beholdeth himself, and goeth his way, and straightway forgetteth what manner of man he was.

25 But whoso looketh into the perfect law of liberty, and continueth therein, he being not a forgetful hearer, but a doer of the work, this man shall be blessed in his deed.

26 If any man among you seem to be religious, and bridleth not his tongue, but deceiveth his own heart, this man's religion is vain.

27 Pure religion and undefiled before God and the Father is this, To visit the fatherless and widows in their affliction, and to keep himself unspotted from the world.

■ THE LESSON EXPLAINED

Faith in Trials (vv. 1–12)

Where has the joy gone? Why is life so routine and boring? The preacher says to stick in there and do what the Bible teaches. Everybody else says forget the preacher and come, have a good time. What am I to do? If I obey the Bible, I lose friends. I may even have to lose my job, for you know what the boss expects.

James wrote to people in worse shape than you. Obeying God brought persecution. Not open, life-threatening persecution that could make you a martyr and hero. They faced subtle discrimination. Jews did not like them, for they had betrayed the national religion. Romans did not like them because they did not belong to a recognized religion and did not tolerate Roman lifestyles or Roman religion. Christians could not find jobs, could not gain social or political recognition, and felt looked down on and discriminated against. Many people can quickly describe the feelings of James's audience.

James had a quick word for them: keep the faith. Let God, not popularity, bring joy. Be patient and see how obedience to God leaves you feeling in the long run.

Patience requires something I do not seem to have. Yes, that requires wisdom to choose God's way and not human ways. Such wisdom has only one source—God. Pray for wisdom. No, do not just say the words and expect miracles to happen. Pray! Trust God totally. Trust Him to work out things in His way in His timing. No, do not go to God for a while and then back to the world for a while. Stay with God totally and always. No, do not think you have to get rich and earn the right to pray. Depend on God to lift you up, not on riches or people or politics. Riches fade. God's rewards do not. Trust God even in the darkest moment.

Faith in Temptation (vv. 13–18)

No, do not scapegoat God. I am not saying God is causing all the troubles you have and thus tempting you to follow the world. God never tries to get you to do wrong. That would mean God is doing wrong. He never does wrong. Temptation comes because you neglect God and follow your own human ways. Human ways follow lust. Lust leads to sin. Sin sends you to death. You want good things, not bad; life, not death. Depend on God. He alone gives good things. Every good thing comes from Him. Trust Him.

Faith in Teaching (vv. 19–27)

You expect the impossible. Follow God always. Neglect my human wishes completely? How can I possibly do that? Simple! Read God's Word. Obey it. Concentrate on God, and ignore the hungers of the flesh. Simply put: shut your mouth and listen to God. Give up pride, and meekly let God shape your life. Quit just going to church on Sunday and listening to the preacher. Read the Word yourself, and do something about it. Obey the Bible! You forget what you merely hear once. You remember what you read and obey. How do I know I am obeying? Listen to what you say. Your tongue reveals your heart. Disobedient tongues show bad religion. Then pass one more test. How do you spend your time: trying to get rich or helping the helpless? Which did Jesus do? Follow Him.

■ TRUTHS TO LIVE BY

Faith and trials are life-long partners. You obey either God or the world. You face trials in the world or eternal judgment. Take your choice.

Faith never focuses on temptation. Faith looks to God and His Word for direction. Temptation comes when you focus on the world and its pleasures.

Faith reads the Word and ministers. Faith does not measure life by economic prosperity or social popularity. Faith measures life by knowledge of God's Word and application of the Word to unhappy lives.

■ A VERSE TO REMEMBER

The trying of our faith worketh patience, but let patience have her perfect work, that ye may be perfect and entire, wanting nothing.—James 1:3–4

■ DAILY BIBLE READINGS

May 27 — The Supremacy of God's Wisdom. Job 28:12–23
May 28 — Confident of Being Heard. 1 John 5:13–21
May 29 — God's Eternity, Man's Transience. Ps. 90:1–6
May 30 — Compassionate Warning. Heb. 12:3–11
May 31 — Sharing God's Good News. 1 Tim. 1:3–12
June 1 — Wholehearted Trust. Prov. 3:5–12
June 2 — Alive in Christ. Rom. 6:5–14

Faith and Relationships

JAMES 2:1-13; 4:11-12

Paul was so kind. From the first time we entered the German-speaking church, he welcomed us, treated us kindly, and waited patiently as we tried to learn German so we could communicate better with him. Paul made us feel like Christian family in every way. Later, I found one thing separated us from Paul, and that was his enormous bank account. The world would say we could never be friends. Economic and social status should keep us apart. Paul let Christ say to him, do not be a respecter of persons. We would treat everyone alike.

■ THE BIBLE LESSON

1 My brethren, have not the faith of our Lord Jesus Christ, the Lord of glory, with respect of persons.

2 For if there come unto your assembly a man with a gold ring, in goodly apparel, and there come in also a poor man in vile raiment;

3 And ye have respect to him that weareth the gay clothing, and say unto him, Sit thou here in a good place; and say to the poor, Stand thou there, or sit here under my footstool:

4 Are ye not then partial in yourselves, and are become judges of evil thoughts?

5 Hearken, my beloved brethren, Hath not God chosen the poor of this world rich in faith, and heirs of the kingdom which he hath promised to them that love him?

6 But ye have despised the poor. Do not rich men oppress you, and draw you before the judgment seats?

7 Do not they blaspheme that worthy name by the which ye are called?

8 If ye fulfill the royal law according to the scripture, Thou shalt love thy neighbor as thyself, ye do well:

9 But if ye have respect to persons, ye commit sin, and are convinced of the law as transgressors.

10 For whosoever shall keep the whole law, and yet offend in one point, he is guilty of all.

11 For he that said, Do not commit adultery, said also, Do not kill. Now if thou commit no adultery, yet if thou kill, thou art become a transgressor of the law.

12 So speak ye, and so do, as they that shall be judged by the law of liberty.

13 For he shall have judgment without mercy, that hath showed no mercy; and mercy rejoiceth against judgment.

. . . .

4:11 Speak not evil one of another, brethren. He that speaketh evil of his brother, and judgeth his brother, speaketh evil of the law, and judgeth the law: but if thou judge the law, thou art not a doer of the law, but a judge.

12 There is one lawgiver, who is able to save and to destroy: who art thou that judgest another?

■ THE LESSON EXPLAINED
Faith to Be Blind (2:1–6)

Poor! Words cannot begin to describe the poverty James's audience faced. Most had to find a new job every day. If job-givers discovered they followed Christ, forget it. No job today. Charity cases—that's what they became. Church members who had money supported many who did not. Oh, to get a few more rich members!

Watch out! cried James. You poor people are making riches your god just as you accuse the wealthy of doing. Money can become god no matter how much or how little you have. When money becomes god, money puts life all out of kilter. You especially lose your focus on people.

Personal relationships, friendships, and Christian love and community vanish. Why? You no longer seek to relate to people because of their Christian characteristics of love, care, warmth, joy, and hope. You begin looking at bank accounts. You limit your friends to those who can help you most—loan or give you money, find you a job, push you up the social ladder, get you a promotion. People are no longer equals who share pains and joys, hopes and despairs, good times and bad times. People are tools you use to get what you want. And they use you to get what they want, even if it means taking you to court.

Faith to Love (2:7–13)

What am I supposed to do then? Avoid the rich? Give up all hope of improving myself? Stay poor for life? Yes, and no. If pandering to the rich is the only way to improve yourself and gain the goals you want, then yes, give this up and stay poor. Why? You have the wrong goals. God's kingdom is the goal, not human wealth and success. But, no, you do not necessarily have to give up your goals, if you are willing to use the abilities God gave you, work hard in an honest way, and depend upon Him to lead you to the achievements He wants you to make.

After all, whom did God choose to be part of His kingdom? All those rich people, or you poor ones? Do you trust Him to do what He promised, to bring you the rewards of the kingdom? Then live His way, not the world's. What is God's way? Scripture tells you to love your neighbor as yourself. I know, you want just one little exception. Can't you get by with one little sin? Surely, just trying to get one rich guy to help me is not too bad a sin? That's the way you always think. You classify sins and decide which sins are acceptable. God looks at it a different way. He has no sin classifications. All stand at the top of His list. Any sin you choose, He condemns. Any sin pays sin's constant wages: death.

No, we are not back in a religion of Mosaic law. We are in the religion of the law of love. This law asks only one question. Did you act in this situation with love as God acts with love? Love frees you and the other person to achieve the best they can for God. If you did not act in pure love toward them, then you limited them and yourself. You are guilty before the law of love. You face God's judgment.

Well, I have already committed that sin. I am without hope. I might as well go on and sin and get this world's goods, for I certainly face God's judgment. Wait a minute. God is love. His mercy wins in the end. He is forgiving. Go back to Him for forgiveness and let Him implant His love in you. Trust His mercy. At the same time do not try to trick God by getting away with sins and then going back for more mercy. God expects you to form love relationships with people just as He forms a love relationship with you. If love does not dominate your life and your relationships, then the wages of your sin is death.

Faith Cannot Speak (4:11–12)

Faith acts in positive love, but sometimes faith refuses to act. Faith does not join gossip sessions, pity parties, and trash-talking moments. Love respects the reputations of other people. Love refuses to speak when the words that would come out would hurt someone else. Why? Faith follows the law of love. To say bad things about another person shows love neither to the person nor to the people you speak to.

Bad talk about people thus breaks the law of love. That means you do not really take the law of love seriously. You want to pick and choose when you follow it and when you do not. This means you do not trust the One who gave you the law of love. Instead, you have set yourself up as a judge who decides when the law applies and when it does not. That means you have put yourself in place of God, for God is the only person who has the right to establish laws for living in His universe and who has the right to judge people for not following His law of love.

Do you really want to stand before Him and say, I chose to ignore the law of love in this case for that person really did something bad. Are you sure? Let God judge the other person. You look into the law of love and see if it describes what you are doing. If your words are not words of love, have the faith to be quiet.

■ TRUTHS TO LIVE BY

Faith trusts God, not riches. Partiality to other people means you want something from them more than you want what God has promised. Your relationships with other people mirror your faith or lack of it.

Faith is judged by its love. God gives you one law: love. He judges you with one test: do you act and speak in love? Salvation is God's love relationship with you that creates His love in your heart. Faith lets that love flow through you to all other people, no matter if they can help you or harm you.

Faith knows when to be silent. Faith keeps silent when words would hurt someone else. Silence often shows love better than words ever could.

■ A VERSE TO REMEMBER

If ye fulfill the royal law according to the scripture, Thou shalt love thy neighbor as thyself, ye do well.—James 2:8

■ DAILY BIBLE READINGS

June 3 — No Room for Boasting. 1 Cor. 1:26–31
June 4 — Just Treatment. Lev. 19:15–19
June 5 — Divine Disapproval. Deut. 27:15–26
June 6 — Moral Qualities. Ps. 15:1–5
June 7 — Abuse Not Your Liberty. Gal. 5:13–25
June 8 — Following Christ's Attitude. Phil. 2:1–11
June 9 — Proper Restraint. Rom. 14:10–23

Faith and Action

JAMES 2:14-26; 5:7-20

He was an old man when I met him. A lonely man with few abilities that anyone saw. But he was a stubbornly dedicated man. He never drove a car, as far as I knew. He just walked miles and miles doing good for his town, the farm people who lived around him, and his church. I saw him in action every Sunday morning, even when it snowed a foot. Still, he plodded the three miles through the early morning weather to church, an hour before even the preacher managed to walk across the road to the church. Quickly, he walked to the bell tower and began pulling the rope. Ringing the bell was his way of calling people to worship. He knew his personal limits, but he ignored them to do whatever he could to invite people to his Lord.

■ THE BIBLE LESSON

14 What doth it profit, my brethren, though a man say he hath faith, and have not works? can faith save him?

15 If a brother or sister be naked, and destitute of daily food,

16 And one of you say unto them, Depart in peace, be ye warmed and filled; notwithstanding ye give them not those things which are needful to the body; what doth it profit?

17 Even so faith, if it hath not works, is dead, being alone.

18 Yea, a man may say, Thou hast faith, and I have works: show me thy faith without thy works, and I will show thee my faith by my works.

19 Thou believest that there is one God; thou doest well: the devils also believe, and tremble.

20 But wilt thou know, O vain man, that faith without works is dead?

21 Was not Abraham our father justified by works, when he had offered Isaac his son upon the altar?

22 Seest thou how faith wrought with his works, and by works was faith made perfect?

23 And the scripture was fulfilled which saith, Abraham believed God, and it was imputed unto him for righteousness: and he was called the

Friend of God.

24 Ye see then how that by works a man is justified, and not by faith only.

25 Likewise also was not Rahab the harlot justified by works, when she had received the messengers, and had sent them out another way?

26 For as the body without the spirit is dead, so faith without works is dead also.

. . . .

5:13 Is any among you afflicted? let him pray. Is any merry? let him sing psalms.

14 Is any sick among you? let him call for the elders of the church; and let them pray over him, anointing him with oil in the name of the Lord:

15 And the prayer of faith shall save the sick, and the Lord shall raise him up; and if he have committed sins, they shall be forgiven him.

16 Confess your faults one to another, and pray one for another, that ye may be healed. The effectual fervent prayer of a righteous man availeth much.

■ THE LESSON EXPLAINED

Faith That Lives (2:14–20)

Why does *faith* seem like such an invisible word to me? Preachers talk about it all the time but they just cannot paint a picture I see. They convince me to join the church and say I have faith. But do I really? How can I be sure?

James thundered forth at a church that had no pictures of faith. He painted a picture quickly of one homeless, hungry person. How do you react? That is the test of faith. Do you start condemning the person, ruining the person's self-confidence and reputation even more? Or do you let faith's tongue be silent and faith's hands and feet spring into action? Faith without food for the hungry is not faith. Jesus warned us of the surprise waiting for many of us at the last judgment (Matt. 25). Remember, "Inasmuch as ye have done it unto one of the least of these my brethren, ye have done it unto me" (v. 40).

But Paul kept saying faith, not works. Is James now telling us to go to work to have faith? Oh, no. Do not get the cart in front of the horse. James agrees with Paul. You can never earn your way to salvation. God does not keep a chart to see if you have done five more good things than bad things. One sin earns the wages of death. God just has a stronger definition of saving faith than we may want Him to have. God says faith that trusts in Christ for salvation is faith that obeys Christ in daily life. Faith is not a one-time statement that then rests on its laurels until the judgment. Faith is a life-long commitment to represent Christ on earth, living as Christ lived—on behalf of the underprivileged and hopeless.

Faith is more than accepting knowledge. Satan passes the knowledge test. Only one God exists. Satan knows that. Satan cannot pass the living test. He disobeys God at every turn. Does your life look like Satan's—or like Jesus'? That is the test of faith.

Faith That Saves (2:21–26)

I thought Abraham was the test case. God told him something. Abraham believed what God said. God declared Abraham righteous or saved. Genesis 11 and 12 show us what faith is. Right? Exactly. Abraham is the Old Testament's prime example of faith. But look how faith lived in Abraham's life years later. God told him to take the promised son of his old age and put him on the altar as a sacrificial lamb to God. Abraham obeyed. (See Gen. 22.)

An even stranger example of justifying, living faith? Look at Joshua 2. The Canaanite harlot Rahab hears of what God has done for Israel. Two strangers appear at her door, probably not an overly strange occurrence. She recognizes them as Israelites and risks her life to protect them even when the king ruling her country orders her to do otherwise. Putting your life on the line for God—that is faith.

Look at it this way. You see a body at the funeral home. Something is missing. That is not a person. It is a corpse. It is the same way with faith. A person who never obeys God, never does anything just because God said do it—That person is spiritually dead, earning sin's wages. He has no faith to give life. Living, justifying faith works for God!

Faith That Expects (5:7–20)

How long do I have to have faith? Payday never seems to

come. What do I get out of it? What do you expect to get out of it? What promises has God made to you? Farmers have to wait a long time for crops. Prophets suffered a long time without seeing God fulfill their message. Job suffered more than anyone can imagine before God answered him. God never promised immediate gratification. He said, get your hearts right. Don't hold grudges. Don't want what someone else already has. Do not make oaths you may never be able to keep. Trust God and His timing.

What do I do while I wait? Pray to God for help. Find other people who need God's power. Pray for God to heal them. Find those who need forgiveness. Lead them to the One who can forgive. Meet with your church; confess your sins; pray for each other. Expect God to answer your prayers like He did Elijah's. All the while, expect God to fulfill the promises He has made and to come as He has said He would. The wait will not seem long if you are busy doing what Jesus would do. Want an exciting life? Learn to wait for God. While you wait, act as He does.

■ TRUTHS TO LIVE BY

Faith is always working. Faith is not idle meditation. Faith is finding God at work in this world and joining Him in His work. Idleness opens sin's door. Working with God shows faith's door is open wide.

Faith saves and changes lives. A life of faith changes radically from life before or without faith. Focus shifts from self to God. Actions shift from selfish to selfless. Emotions move from fear and frustration to hope and joy. Saving faith finds ways to show salvation in action to those who doubt or do not know faith.

Faith waits. Faith needs no further proof. God is at work in the life of faith. Faith willingly waits for God's time to act. Faith needs rewards only when God is ready to give them. Meanwhile, faith actively waits by serving and praying.

■ A VERSE TO REMEMBER

For as the body without the spirit is dead, so faith without works is dead also.—James 2:26

■ DAILY BIBLE READINGS

Faith and Wisdom

JAMES 1:5-8; 3:1-5A,13-18

The Germans called him Herr Professor Doktor, Doktor, Doktor. He had earned three doctor's degrees. I knew several men like him, with more education than 99 percent of the world's population. Still, forced to ask for the wisest people I knew, I might well point to some residents of a rural town in Tennessee. They had little schooling, but lots of education. They said little but helped much. They spoke softly but listened loudly.

When the world went wrong, I went to this deacon and his wife. They could not match my education, but had ever so much more wisdom. While I listened to teachers, they listened to people. They knew how people felt, thought, responded, and hoped. I poured out hundreds of words of woe. They replied with a few well-chosen words of hope. Their living room was the finest school I ever attended.

■ THE BIBLE LESSON

5 *If any of you lack wisdom, let him ask of God, that giveth to all men liberally, and upbraideth not; and it shall be given him.*

6 *But let him ask in faith, nothing wavering. For he that wavereth is like a wave of the sea driven with the wind and tossed.*

7 *For let not that man think that he shall receive any thing of the Lord.*

8 *A double-minded man is unstable in all his ways.*

. . . .

3:1 *My brethren, be not many masters, knowing that we shall receive the greater condemnation.*

2 *For in many things we offend all. If any man offend not in word, the same is a perfect man, and able also to bridle the whole body.*

3 *Behold, we put bits in the horses' mouths, that they may obey us; and we turn about their whole body.*

4 *Behold also the ships, which though they be so great, and are driven of fierce winds, yet are they turned about with a very small helm, whithersoever the governor listeth.*

5 *Even so the tongue is a little member, and boasteth great things.*

. . . .

13 *Who is a wise man and endued with knowledge among you? let him show out of a good conversation his works with meekness of wisdom.*

14 *But if ye have bitter envying and strife in your hearts, glory not, and lie not against the truth.*

15 *This wisdom descendeth not from above, but is earthly, sensual, devilish.*

16 *For where envying and strife is, there is confusion and every evil work.*

17 *But the wisdom that is from above is first pure, then peaceable, gentle, and easy to be entreated, full of mercy and good fruits, without partiality, and without hypocrisy.*

18 *And the fruit of righteousness is sown in peace of them that make peace.*

■ THE LESSON EXPLAINED

Wisdom's Source: Faithful Prayer (1:5–8)

With two children, a traveling job, and little money, my father-in-law faced many problems. He had one solution. While others slept, he fell to his knees beside his bed and prayed. I still miss his prayers. They lifted my wife and me through many hard moments. He knew James's lesson. Pray it through. A problem has a solution, but only God knows it. God does not selfishly hoard the solutions to our problems. He waits until we unswervingly ask Him for His wisdom. Then He shows us how to solve the problem. Praying for help and looking for the world to provide a solution at the same time does not work. Drop all else. Drop to your knees. Pray. Know God will answer. And He will—only, however, if you trust Him and only Him.

Wisdom's Results: A Tamed Tongue (3:1–12)

For over a decade I dared mount the professor's rostrum to teach young adults how to do God's work. James warned against that. Few of us have the one quality God requires of a teacher—a tamed tongue. Show God is in control of your life by showing He controls your tongue. The tongue may be small. So is a bit in a horse's mouth and a rudder on a ship. These small items exercise total control.

In many ways the tongue has even more control. Children may not obey the words, but they echo the emotions our tongues utter. Friends and enemies form opinions of us by the way we operate our tongues. Satan uses our tongue to destroy the reputations of others and in so doing our own. A word falsely chosen splits our church, enflames our family, and denies us any opportunity to witness for God.

What poison does your tongue contain? What evil does it cause? Is it among the species that are wild or tamed? Do you pray and praise on Sunday and then curse and condemn others on Monday? This is not God's way! You claim to be a fig tree but produce olives? You claim to issue the fresh word of life as you teach, but it sounds like old salt to the listeners? Ask God for wisdom to tame the tongue.

Wisdom's Test: Peace Among People (3:13–18)

I know so much, but people just will not listen! Wonder why? How do people hear you? As a voice of strife, trying to change everyone's life? A call of envy seeking to have what someone else has earned? A braggart forgetting the accomplishments of others? A liar twisting facts to enhance yourself? Why are you heard in this way? Because you adopt the world's values and seek the world's kind of rewards? Because Satan's way appeals to you more than God's?

Are you in the middle of battle with other people? Does envy surround what you are doing? Stop. Ask one question. What is the source of such confusion? The Bible has one plain answer. Such confusion comes only from Satan. God never causes fights, envy, or confusion.

What does God cause? He is wisdom's source. He tames your tongue. He brings pure thoughts, peaceful relationships, gentle words, willingness to listen and follow others' advice, love, and mercy that help others. God's wisdom leads you away from partiality, favoritism, and special interest groups. God's wisdom speaks with sincerity, creating words others can trust with no reason to doubt your truthfulness or your motives. In one word. God is the cause of peace. If you have faith, letting God's love live in and through you, then peace is the result of your life. If you cause anything but peace, it is time for a faith checkup. Ask God for wisdom. He gives it liberally.

■ TRUTHS TO LIVE BY

Wisdom comes only from God. Humans can create knowledge. Wisdom knows how to use knowledge. Only God can show you that. Ask God for the wisdom and love to use what you know to benefit other people.

Wisdom does not have to talk. Actions show wisdom more than words. Actions stem from the Spirit God has placed in your heart. Let the Spirit of wisdom control and tame your tongue.

Wisdom creates peace. Wise words never lead to war. Wise words calm ruffled feelings. Ask God for wisdom to bring peace when all signs signal the battle cry.

■ A VERSE TO REMEMBER

Who is a wise man and endued with knowledge among you? let him shew out of a good conversation his works with meekness of wisdom.— James 3:13

■ DAILY BIBLE READINGS

June 17 — Wisdom Granted by God. Job 28:12–22,28
June 18 — Messiah's Spirit of Wisdom. Isa. 11:1–5
June 19 — Surprised by His Wisdom. Matt. 13:53–58
June 20 — Wisdom of Obedience. Matt. 7:21–28
June 21 — Superior Wisdom in Committed Lives.
              Dan. 1:17–21
June 22 — Faith Begets Wisdom from Above. 1 Cor. 2:1–8
June 23 — Folly of Worldly Wisdom. 1 Cor. 3:16–23

Faith and Righteousness

JAMES 4:1-10,13-17

He had everything you could desire—good looking, talented, in demand around the nation for his leadership and entertainment skills, wealthy parents, a beautiful, wealthy wife. All this with a heart of gold, for he was willing to help anyone who came along. Church and charities depended on him whenever they did something for the poor and needy.

But something was missing. The lean body grew fat. The talents began to disappear because he no longer used them. The wife divorced him. The parents refused to supply money to be wasted on alcohol. Despair, despondency, anger, and self-pity took over. Why? James knew.

■ THE BIBLE LESSON

1 From whence come wars and fightings among you? come they not hence, even of your lusts that war in your members?

2 Ye lust, and have not: ye kill, and desire to have, and cannot obtain: ye fight and war, yet ye have not, because ye ask not.

3 Ye ask, and receive not, because ye ask amiss, that ye may consume it upon your lusts.

4 Ye adulterers and adulteresses, know ye not that the friendship of the world is enmity with God? whosoever therefore will be a friend of the world is the enemy of God.

5 Do ye think that the scripture saith in vain, The spirit that dwelleth in us lusteth to envy?

6 But he giveth more grace. Wherefore he saith, God resisteth the proud, but giveth grace unto the humble.

7 Submit yourselves therefore to God. Resist the devil, and he will flee from you.

8 Draw nigh to God, and he will draw nigh to you. Cleanse your hands, ye sinners; and purify your hearts, ye double-minded.

9 *Be afflicted, and mourn, and weep: let your laughter be turned to mourning, and your joy to heaviness.*

10 *Humble yourselves in the sight of the Lord, and he shall lift you up.*

. . . .

13 *Go to now, ye that say, To day or tomorrow we will go into such a city, and continue there a year, and buy and sell, and get gain:*

14 *Whereas ye know not what shall be on the morrow. For what is your life? It is even a vapor, that appeareth for a little time, and then vanisheth away.*

15 *For that ye ought to say, If the Lord will, we shall live, and do this, or that.*

16 *But now ye rejoice in your boastings: all such rejoicing is evil.*

17 *Therefore to him that knoweth to do good, and doeth it not, to him it is sin.*

■ THE LESSON EXPLAINED

Enemy of Righteousness: Lust (vv. 1–5)

Two forces fight for you: righteousness and lust. God and His righteousness fight against the world and its lustful envy. Lust has one goal: control everything you see. Lust has no limits: do anything necessary to get what you want. Lust has no religion: it never prays for God's will to be done, only for more things to be given. Lust has no relationship with God: only a friendship with the world seeking to get what the world seems to possess (compare 2:23). Lust has no commitments: vows to God vanish in adulterous relationships with the world.

How can we be sure of this? James says that the Bible tells us so. James just does not tell us where the Bible tells us so, and many translators would say James does not really tell us exactly what the Bible says. Before making definite statements about verse 5, you need to compare as many translations as possible. Apparently, James used the Old Testament teaching that God is a jealous God (Exod. 34:14). That jealous Spirit of God opposes anything that takes His place in our life. Lust and worldly ways take God's place in our lives. God puts His jealous Spirit in us to do away with the lust and envy of the world.

The Way of Righteousness: Humility (vv. 6–12)

What hope do we have then? We can humbly trust in Him, for He gives grace to the humble to resist all pride and envy. But that means I lose all control. I am not in charge. Exactly. You never have been. Either God controls your life, or Satan does. You make the choice. Do you follow Satan, or will you fight him? You do so only in one way: draw near to God; experience Him in obedience. Grieve over your own death, for you have received the wages of sin. Forsake the world's kind of joy and laughter. Quit trying to lift yourselves up by your own bootstraps. Let God lift you up. Quit trying to gain an advantage over other people by condemning them. Trust God to save you and to judge those who oppose Him. Humbled before God, you cannot judge someone else.

The Uncertainty of Righteousness: End Time (vv. 13–17)

Lust, pride, and envy—Satan's tools in our lives—produce certainty. We predict what will happen tomorrow and promise what we will do years from now. We count our profits before we buy a cash register. God calls to holy uncertainty. Remember life is short in the long run. We have no control. Only God knows how long we will live. All plans must face His approval. You have heard His Word. You know what He expects in His law of love. You know how to do good. Will you continue in your boasting ways? Beware! You know what to do. When you refuse to do it, you sin. You know sin's wages. Is that the paycheck you want? No? Then do everything in humble prayer before God, letting Him show His work and His ways. Then when your vapor vanishes, eternal life will continue.

■ TRUTHS TO LIVE BY

Lust leaves no assets. What your heart wants controls you. Your heart faces two offers: Satan's lusts and God's righteousness. Lust may bring momentary treasures, but they disappear with the vapor of life. Righteousness promises eternal life.

Humility seeks no assets. Humility is lust's opposite. Humility trusts God for everything in life. Experiencing God through obedience satisfies humility's desires. Worldly assets offer no allure to humility's love.

Eternity ends all material assets. Your time frame determines your life. Focus on today seeks riches, wealth, security, and social acceptance. Focus on eternity seeks love and eternal life. How are you focused?

■ A VERSE TO REMEMBER

Therefore to him that knoweth to do good, and doeth it not, to him it is sin.—James 4:17

■ DAILY BIBLE READINGS

June 24 — Assured of Innocence. Job 27:1–11
June 25 — Worthy Resolves. Ps. 66:13–20
June 26 — A True Relationship. 1 John 2:12–17
June 27 — An Expression of Faith. Ps. 138:1–8
June 28 — Blessings of the Righteous. Prov. 3:27–35
June 29 — Trust in God's Grace. Isa. 55:6–11
June 30 — Qualified to Enter God's Presence. Ps. 24:1–6

Praising God as Creator and Sustainer

PSALM 104

Four hours in an old school bus with fifty people over almost nonexistent roads quickly destroyed my tourist's enthusiasm and my patience. One turn in the road made it all worth while, however. Majestically raising its twin peaks twenty thousand feet above ground, Mount McKinley turned my mind away from my woes to His worth. Only a Creator God could plan and produce such a monument to His glory. Before I pulled out my camera to record a small bit of its beauty, I fell to my knees to thank and praise Him for this moment of awe before His beauty.

■ THE BIBLE LESSON

24 O Lord, how manifold are thy works! in wisdom hast thou made them all: the earth is full of thy riches.

25 So is this great and wide sea, wherein are things creeping innumerable, both small and great beasts.

26 There go the ships: there is that leviathan, whom thou hast made to play therein.

27 These wait all upon thee; that thou mayest give them their meat in due season.

28 That thou givest them they gather: thou openest thine hand, they are filled with good.

29 Thou hidest thy face, they are troubled: thou takest away their breath, they die, and return to their dust.

30 Thou sendest forth thy spirit, they are created: and thou renewest the face of the earth.

31 The glory of the Lord shall endure forever: the Lord shall rejoice in his works.

32 He looketh on the earth, and it trembleth: he toucheth the hills, and they smoke.

33 I will sing unto the Lord as long as I live: I will sing praise to my

God while I have my being.
34 My meditation of him shall be sweet: I will be glad in the Lord.

■ THE LESSON EXPLAINED

Creation: Planned for Every Creature (vv. 1–23)

Why am I alive? The Psalmist did not have to pause to answer. I live to bless God with all He has created me to be. How can I do this? Admire His creation, and let the praises ring. See God sovereign and in control of everything in this world. See the sturdy nature of the world able to endure through all the ages. See God's power over the fearful ocean deeps with all their strange and fearful creatures. Note the forceful rivers confined to the banks God built for them, never again to flood the world. See how those powerful rivers peacefully give drink to the wildest of animals. See how they provide trees as a home for the birds. Thrill at the beauty of earth's green bounty. Partake of the food God causes to grow for you.

Accept God's gifts with gladness. Use His products to enhance your beauty. Look unto the hills where only the surefooted animals can roam, unthreatened by preying beasts unable to climb the heights after them. Enjoy the seasons controlled by the moon. Be astonished at the power of God to manage the brilliance, heat, and explosive power of the sun. No wonder the ancients worshiped sun rather than Father. Fear not as darkness falls. Let it serve its function of covering the predators as they seek the prey they have need to exist. Use the day to accomplish the work God sets before you.

Creation: Providing for Every Creature (vv. 24–30)

How can I stay alive? Each day brings new threats. Will I have a job? Can I provide for my family? Will I face critical surgery, injury, or disease? I just do not know what tomorrow will bring. How can I retain hope and praise God in such an uncertain world?

Faith paints a different picture. Life may be uncertain, but God remains a certainty. Life is worth it all, for life offers a peek into God's majesty and wisdom. Life previews God's rich treasure chest, open to meet the needs He knows I have. O, yes, Lord of life, You are indescribably great. I will bless You with all You have made me to be! I will trust You to supply all my needs. I place all my tomorrows in Your certain hands. Why?

I see the miracle of the seas where whales, sharks, and minnows exist together. I see great cargo ships arrive safely despite the threat of huge sea monsters the old sailors keep telling us about. What a God You are to create a playpen for sea monsters. As big as they are, they eat only because You provide for them. In all their power, they live only because You provide them the breath of life, just as You provide it for me. They, and I, would die should You turn Your back on us. Oh, yes, only You are the source of life. I can depend on You! So I bless Your name.

Creation: Revealing God's Eternal Glory (vv. 31–34)

Where is the end of all of this? Can such glorious beauty and symmetry last forever? Will God's rich bounty always stand at our disposal? The answer can come only from God. He is the Eternal One. His glory lasts forever. The earth lasts because it brings joy to the Creator. He sees His works and rejoices. He even comes to it and shows His power in the earthquakes and erupting volcanoes. Still the earth endures.

No more questions. I see my purpose. I will sing praises to God as long as He lets me live. Questions will no longer trouble me. I will show a sweet spirit as I sing His praises. I will let Him make me glad. He will take care of everything that threatens what He has made. Sinners and wicked people stand no chance. He controls their destiny just as He controls mine. I will praise God. Everyone join in. Praise the LORD!

■ TRUTHS TO LIVE BY

Earthly beauty reveals eternal Glory. Earth's majesty says little about human power. It reveals volumes to faith about God's glorious sovereignty.

Earthly order points beyond temporary disorder. Human eyes easily focus on problems and fears. God's order in earth and sea and sky points beyond troubles of the moment to triumphs of the Eternal. Troubles vanish when God comes into full view.

Earth's end only leads you on into eternity. You are mortal. Death comes inevitably. Still you can praise God, for He has promised you eternity with Him. If earth seems to reveal greatness, what will heaven provide?

■ A VERSE TO REMEMBER

O LORD, how manifold are thy works! in wisdom hast thou made them all: the earth is full of thy riches.
—Psalm 104:24

■ DAILY BIBLE READINGS

July 1 — The Lord as Creator. Ps. 33:1–9
July 2 — Creation by God's Word. Gen. 1:1–8
July 3 — Separation of Land and Water. Gen. 1:9–13
July 4 — Celestial Bodies Provide Light. Gen. 1:14–19
July 5 — Animals Indirectly Related to God. Gen. 1:20–25
July 6 — People to Dominate the Earth. Gen. 1:26–31
July 7 — Made to Need Each Other. Gen. 2:18–24

Praising God for Mighty Acts

PSALM 105

See what God has done for you, he said. You really did not expect this, did you? Again my sainted father-in-law 's faith received rewards even when doubts blinded me. It was a simple thing. We had been married only a year. Dad Burnett promised to take us to Miami for the annual meeting of our denomination. We so looked forward to it.

Then we passed the majestic motels with their ocean views and came to the small place where we could afford to stay. We stumbled down its threadbare carpets, looking at its rooms to see their strained views of the ocean. Turning the corner, we appeared to leave the ocean behind. Entering the room, our fears were realized. We saw no windows on the ocean, only a small, dark, dreary room.

Then Dad stepped away for a minute and found the string. One pull placed a magnificent window before us. Beyond stood the mighty Atlantic in all its glory. God provided a glorious setting for a wonderful week. And we expected so little.

■ THE BIBLE LESSON

1 *O give thanks unto the Lord; call upon his name: make known his deeds among the people.*

2 *Sing unto him, sing psalms unto him: talk ye of all his wondrous works.*

3 *Glory ye in his holy name: let the heart of them rejoice that seek the Lord.*

4 *Seek the Lord, and his strength: seek his face evermore.*

5 *Remember his marvelous works that he hath done; his wonders, and the judgments of his mouth;*

6 *O ye seed of Abraham his servant, ye children of Jacob his chosen.*

7 *He is the Lord our God: his judgments are in all the earth.*

8 He hath remembered his covenant forever, the word which he commanded to a thousand generations.

9 Which covenant he made with Abraham, and his oath unto Isaac;

10 And confirmed the same unto Jacob for a law, and to Israel for an everlasting covenant:

11 Saying, Unto thee will I give the land of Canaan the lot of your inheritance:

. . . .

43 And he brought forth his people with joy, and his chosen with gladness:

44 And gave them the lands of the heathen: and they inherited the labor of the people;

45 That they might observe his statutes, and keep his laws. Praise ye the Lord.

■ THE LESSON EXPLAINED

God's Acts: Reason for Thanksgiving (vv. 1–8)

Hymns sound forth praises for who God is. Thanksgivings respond joyfully to what God has done. Worship includes both. Psalm 104 is a hymn inviting people to praise. Psalm 105 is a thanksgiving reviewing the marvels of God's history with His people. God acts in history to deliver His people so they can tell others what He did. Thanksgiving is the way you share the message in public worship. As you give thanks, you seek God's presence in your life and commit yourself to let His acts continue to control your life. Memory leads to commitment. Memory shows God has been faithful to His covenant promises and calls you to the same faithfulness.

God's History: Sign of Faithfulness (vv. 9–37)

God does not work secretively, hiding His ways, His purposes, and His plans from you. God tells you what He is going to do, and then He faithfully does it. Israel had this lesson indelibly stamped in their memory. God called Abraham, promised to make him a great nation and give him a great land. Then God let decades pass, seemingly inactive and forgetful. He repeated the promise to Isaac and Jacob but seemed to do so little. He did protect them from kings like Abimelech when they lost faith and lied to protect their lives. But their lifestyle changed not. Humble shepherds sought grazing places for small animals. Only a burial ground belonged to them. When changes finally came, they were anything but promising.

Young Joseph experienced deception and imprisonment. God interpreted dreams for him but did not fulfill his own. Then suddenly he ruled Egypt, and his family enjoyed the best land the Pharaoh owned. They gained wealth and numbers, but no land. Then power vanished. Israel endured Egyptian hatred.

Finally, God provided Moses. Signs and wonders and punishments on Egypt brought Israel's freedom with possessions. God took His time to do it, but God remembered His promises. God is faithful. Can we wait on His timetable to learn the lesson again?

God's Gifts: Proof of His Grace (vv. 38–45)

Good riddance, said Egypt. They brought nothing good to us. Where are we going? asked Israel, seeing nothing but barren, mountain-studded wilderness lying before them. God knew the way. His cloud revealed it by day; His heavenly fire led by night. But we have no food, Israel complained. Manna and quail appeared from God's bounty. No water, wailed Israel. We will die. From the rock God gushed forth fresh wetness. Why would He do all this for such an insignificant people? He remembered what He had said. Abraham died long before God acted to fulfill the promise. Years and funerals did not dull God's memory. He waited until He was ready. Then He acted. Joy and gladness reigned. Why? A homeless people found a home. Landless people owned territory.

Why? So Israel could be the convenant people, remembering their promise to be God's faithful, obedient, trusting people. O give thanks to God for He is good. O give obedience to God. Be faithful as He is faithful.

■ TRUTHS TO LIVE BY

God has no forgetter. Whatever God says, He does. He may wait beyond your memory, but He will keep His promise. Such a God deserves all your praise and gratitude.

God accomplishes God-sized tasks. Our sin may be expecting too little from God. We search diligently to find one little thing He is doing. Meanwhile, He patiently waits for us to join Him in the enormous work He is doing to provide worldwide redemption.

God acts because He is love. Human strategy never clarifies God's reasons and timing. God may wait until we desperately cry out to Him for help from our wilderness. In His love God will provide what He knows His people need. Is His love enough for you?

■ A VERSE TO REMEMBER

O give thanks unto the LORD; call upon his name; make known his deeds among the people. — Psalm 105:1

■ DAILY BIBLE READINGS

July 8 — Covenant Initiated by God. Gen. 17:1–8
July 9 — A Helper Provided. Exod. 4:10–17
July 10 — Dependent on God's Mercies. Deut. 8:1–10
July 11 — Praise, Prayer, and Confession. Ps. 106:1–12
July 12 — Confident of God's Help. Isa. 26:7–15
July 13 — God's Discipline. Jer. 32:17–25
July 14 — God's Provisions for Humankind. Luke 1:67–79

Praising God for Deliverance

PSALM 34

Not the C word! Anything but that. Yes, the doctor repeated. It is the C word. We had no hint of it when we went in to operate. We thought it was a simple operation with quick recovery. The operation showed us nothing, so I told you everything was all right. The lab showed how human I am. That is why we have laboratories. You are now a cancer patient. We must keep watch on you and check against any recurrence. We think we got it all, but we must be careful. I was wrong once. I could be again.

Why, Lord, why? we prayed. Then help, Lord, help. Then how long, Lord, how long? Finally, we are beginning to pray, "I will bless the LORD at all times. . . . I sought the LORD, and he heard me, and delivered me from all my fears" (Ps. 34:1,4).

■ THE BIBLE LESSON

2 My soul shall make her boast in the Lord: the humble shall hear thereof, and be glad.

3 O magnify the Lord with me, and let us exalt his name together.

4 I sought the Lord, and he heard me, and delivered me from all my fears.

5 They looked unto him, and were lightened: and their faces were not ashamed.

6 This poor man cried, and the Lord heard him, and saved him out of all his troubles.

7 The angel of the Lord encampeth round about them that fear him, and delivereth them.

8 O taste and see that the Lord is good: blessed is the man that trusteth in him.

9 O fear the Lord, ye his saints: for there is no want to them that fear him.

10 The young lions do lack, and suffer hunger: but they that seek the

Lord shall not want any good thing.

. . . .

18 *The Lord is nigh unto them that are of a broken heart; and saveth such as be of a contrite spirit.*

19 *Many are the afflictions of the righteous: but the Lord delivereth him out of them all.*

20 *He keepeth all his bones: not one of them is broken.*

21 *Evil shall slay the wicked: and they that hate the righteous shall be desolate.*

22 *The Lord redeemeth the soul of his servants: and none of them that trust in him shall be desolate.*

■ THE LESSON EXPLAINED

Invitation to Praise (vv. 1–3)

Praise is never a solo event. No one claims a monopoly on praise. God's wonderful acts of deliverance fill us with such awe and joy that we immediately invite friends, neighbors, church family, and whomever else will join in to praise God with us. When we see God act to deliver us from an impossible situation, all other talk vanishes. One subject dominates conversation. Work, play, worship, idle moments share one subject: what God has done for me. Gladness permeates the earth as the earth comes to see what God has done.

Description of Deliverance (vv. 4–6)

When God accomplishes His God-sized work in your life, you have no doubt what He has done. You stand amazed that He would do it, but amazement does not rob you of ability to describe. God healed my cancer. God saved my life in the accident. God restored life when my heart quit beating. God brought me safely home when I totally lost the way. I faced absolute fear, and God took away all my fears. Each situation is different. Each provides you opportunity to tell God what you have seen Him do and then share the message with everyone you meet. From it all comes one common cry, "I cried to God. God heard. God saved me from all the troubles I faced." Why not take a moment to describe to God how He has delivered you.

Lessons of Deliverance (vv. 7–22)

Deliverance calls for more than prayer and testimony. Deliverance teaches us lessons to apply in future situations. The psalmist learned many. God is always present and knows your needs, standing ready to deliver. You need to trust God and Him alone for deliverance. God deserves your reverence, worship, and awe. You have no reason to be in need, for God provides for His people. Deliverance should deliver your life to obedience and away from sin. Language, lifestyle, and life's goals change when you experience God's deliverance. Evil actions appear in all their evilness, and in the light of God's approaching judgment they lose all their attraction. Humility takes life over when God delivers and assures you of God's presence. The future is secure in God's hands.

Praise and worship do not mark the end of response to God's deliverance. Life is changed forever. Trust in Him replaces all fear. Obedience to Him replaces all evil. Hope in Him eliminates all frustrations. I will praise the Lord at all times.

■ TRUTHS TO LIVE BY

My troubles are God's opportunities. Trouble forces me to face my limits. Trouble reminds me God has no limits. Trouble opens me to ask God for help. God hears cries for help and delivers me.

God's deliverance is my call to testify. Deliverance is concrete action in absolute time of need. I can describe every trouble I faced, every fear I trembled about. I can just as easily describe the action God took to overcome my trouble. I describe it to myself, to my God, to my friends, to my church, and to everyone else who will listen. The world needs to hear of God's deliverance.

God's deliverance changes my life. God-sized deliverance is impressive. It does not linger awhile and pass away. Memories embed themselves in my life. Loving obedience and faithful commitment come naturally when God has delivered you.

■ A VERSE TO REMEMBER

The LORD is nigh unto them that are of a broken heart; and saved such as be of a contrite spirit.—Psalm 34:18

■ DAILY BIBLE READINGS

Praising God Who Knows and Cares

PSALM 139

Blood streamed from my head as I rushed into the house to a stunned mother. Ross doesn't like me anymore, I cried. He drove me home with rocks. I haven't done anything. I don't understand why this has to happen to me. So a pre-teenager discovers the injustice of life. Life is not fair, and no one promised it would be. Where do you go when life's unfairness becomes more than you can handle?

The psalmist had an answer.

■ THE BIBLE LESSON

To the chief Musician, A Psalm of David

1 O Lord, thou hast searched me, and known me.

2 Thou knowest my downsitting and mine uprising, thou understandest my thought afar off.

3 Thou compassest my path and my lying down, and art acquainted with all my ways.

4 For there is not a word in my tongue, but, lo, O Lord, thou knowest it altogether.

5 Thou hast beset me behind and before, and laid thine hand upon me.

6 Such knowledge is too wonderful for me; it is high, I cannot attain unto it.

7 Whither shall I go from thy spirit? or whither shall I flee from thy presence?

8 If I ascend up into heaven, thou art there: if I make my bed in hell, behold, thou art there.

9 If I take the wings of the morning, and dwell in the uttermost parts of the sea;

10 Even there shall thy hand lead me, and thy right hand shall hold me.

11 If I say, Surely the darkness shall cover me; even the night shall be light about me.

12 Yea, the darkness hideth not from thee; but the night shineth as the day: the darkness and the light are both alike to thee.

13 For thou hast possessed my reins: thou hast covered me in my mother's womb.

14 I will praise thee; for I am fearfully and wonderfully made: marvelous are thy works; and that my soul knoweth right well.

. . . .

23 Search me, O God, and know my heart: try me, and know my thoughts:

24 And see if there be any wicked way in me, and lead me in the way everlasting.

■ THE LESSON EXPLAINED

Depending on God's Knowledge (vv. 1–6)

Where can I turn when the whole world is against me? Surely, I do not deserve such a fate. Yes, I have done wrong, but nothing to deserve this. David knew the feeling. The man after God's own heart found his own sons gathering armies to rebel against him. God had punished David and forgiven the sin against Bathsheba. Still, misery ruled. One certainty guided David's response. God knew everything. I can take my deepest feelings and wounds to God. God will understand and never be surprised. God knows my actions, my plans, my thoughts, my words. God surrounds everything I do. God is too wonderful for me to understand. I can never be like that, but I am glad He is; for I can take any problem I have to Him even if no one on earth cares or listens.

Depending on the Ever-present Judge (vv. 7–14a)

I've had enough of people telling me what is wrong with me. I will listen to them no longer. I will take my case to God. He is the only judge I will listen to. I might as well take it to Him. I can never hide from Him. Anywhere I would go, He is already there. High and low, far and wide, day or night, distance, depth, and darkness do not detain the Divine. He is everywhere. He always has been, ever since I was conceived in my mother's womb. He knows my conscience, that part buried in the inner depths of my innards.

Again, that means He knows everything. If anybody will declare me innocent, He will. O, thank God that He is everywhere, knows everything, and still cares for me.

Depending on the Plans of the Creator (vv. 14b–18)

Surely God does not intend for my wicked enemies to succeed in their intentions. God has much more in store for me. Ever since He first began creating me as an embryo in my mother's womb, began fitting my bones together, He has had a plan for me. He keeps a book detailing His purpose for the world, and not just for the world, but also for me. That book may include the eternal destiny of people (Dan. 7:10), but it also includes the earthly purposes for me and everyone else God uses in His purposes. He made me. He knows what I can do. He will enable me to do it. Your purposes, your plans, your thoughts—that's what's important to me, Lord. The enemies will not win. I can trust God's plans for me.

Depending on God the Revenger (vv. 19–24)

Wicked enemies are nothing. Put them out of my mind. God will take care of them. I will have nothing else to do with those who say wicked things about God. They violate the commandments, taking Your name in vain. O, I hate them just as You do, God. I am in deep mourning because they oppose You and Your plans.

I will have absolutely nothing to do with them. I totally hate them with Your kind of hatred of everything that is evil and opposed to your plans.

Your enemies are my enemies, God. I will let You prove it. You know everything. Come, search me. Examine my heart with my emotions and motives in it. You will not find one wicked thought there in this situation. I have aligned myself completely with You. The wicked enemy will be here for a short while. Then You will destroy them. I want to stay with You in the way that lasts forever.

■ TRUTHS TO LIVE BY

When life proves unfair, God is near. Christ suffered for being perfect. His followers suffer unfairly as He did. Christ joined the psalmist is seeking God's will no matter where it led, because He trusted God to be with Him. God will be with you in your darkest moments.

When people accuse you, God will excuse you. People love to judge. Quite often, they judge wrongly. Too often you are the person they judge. Judging them does no good. Go to God. He knows your innocence and will defend you.

When wrong rules, God knows and cares. You do not have to prove your case to God and coerce Him to love you. He is already in a love relationship with you and knows all about you. Just trust Him to care for you in your time of trouble.

■ A VERSE TO REMEMBER

Search me, O God, and know my heart: try me, and know my thoughts.—Psalm. 139:23

■ DAILY BIBLE READINGS

July 22 — God Is Mindful of Us. Ps. 115:3–15
July 23 — God Is Aware. Luke 12:1–9
July 24 — God Cares. 1 Pet. 5:6–11
July 25 — God Strengthens. Isa. 41:8–13
July 26 — God Perseveres. Isa. 46:3–11
July 27 — God Sees All. Heb. 4:1–13
July 28 — God Elicits Confidence. Rom. 8:26–35

Trust in God

PSALM 40

Will I ever learn? God has saved me and my family so many times from wrecks, attempted airplane bombings, being alone and lost in a communist country on May Day unable even to read the train signs, and so many other occasions. Life seems to be a series of my getting into trouble and God delivering. I constantly have to say thank you for all He has done. Then I get in trouble and have to learn the lesson all over again. Why? David gave a one-word answer: Trust!

■ THE BIBLE LESSON

To the chief Musician, A Psalm of David

1 I waited patiently for the Lord; and he inclined unto me, and heard my cry.

2 He brought me up also out of an horrible pit, out of the miry clay, and set my feet upon a rock, and established my goings.

3 And he hath put a new song in my mouth, even praise unto our God: many shall see it, and fear, and shall trust in the Lord.

4 Blessed is that man that maketh the Lord his trust, and respecteth not the proud, nor such as turn aside to lies.

5 Many, O Lord my God, are thy wonderful works which thou hast done, and thy thoughts which are to us–ward: they cannot be reckoned up in order unto thee: if I would declare and speak of them, they are more than can be numbered.

. . . .

9 I have preached righteousness in the great congregation: lo, I have not refrained my lips, O Lord, thou knowest.

10 I have not hid thy righteousness within my heart; I have declared thy faithfulness and thy salvation: I have not concealed thy loving–kindness and thy truth from the great congregation.

11 Withhold not thou thy tender mercies from me, O Lord: let thy loving–kindness and thy truth continually preserve me.

. . . .

16 Let all those that seek thee rejoice and be glad in thee: let such as love thy salvation say continually, The Lord be magnified.

■ THE LESSON EXPLAINED

Trouble Recalls Past Thanksgiving (vv. 1–5)

I'm in trouble again. I can't get out. What do I do now? Calm down. What happened last time? I prayed to God. I waited patiently for Him to answer. He paid attention. He heard me. He got me out of the toughest spot I had ever been in. I sang His praises as I had never sung them before. God used my testimony to show others how to trust Him and worship Him. O, what happiness comes to the person who trusts in God, especially in time of trouble.

I learned the lesson that time. I have to trust God. All these people with their plans for success don't help me when I need them. They are too proud of what they are doing to bother about me. God is the only One who accomplishes the God-sized work it takes to get me out of my troubles. I can't even list all that He has done. Certainly no one on earth compares. He cares for me as no one else. Why don't I trust Him more?

Trouble Teaches Us to Testify (vv. 6–10)

What can I do for God? He has delivered me so many times, and now I need Him again. What can I do? Promising to give something to the church is not the answer. I am already doing that. David could look into God's Book in Deuteronomy and find rules for the king. I can look in the Bible and find directions God has for me to obey Him. I am willing to do all that He asks. I want to obey Him totally. He has put His teaching in my heart so that I both know it and want to follow it. More than that! I teach it at church. I show others how to obey God. I have told everyone all that You have done to deliver me. God, is that not trusting You? What more can I do?

Trouble Is Time for Talk with God (vv. 11–17)

Where is God? If He is the all-loving, merciful One, where is He when I need Him? O, God, quit keeping Your love and mercy to Yourself. Share it with me. I need it badly. Enemies surround me and persecute me. I still seem to be paying for all those horrible sins of my past. I am heartbroken, bent over with grief and sadness. Hurry up, God. Come help me. Get my enemies. Put them to shame. They have called me names and made fun of me. Take everything away from them so they will deserve the names they called me.

But, God, not everyone is like that. Thanks be to You, many people rejoice in You and find gladness in worshiping You. Bless them, God. Give them reason to praise You. Right now, though, it is hard for me. I am in too much trouble. You are the only hope I have. You always have helped me and delivered me. Do it again, Lord. Now, Lord. Okay, I have had my say. I will go back to the beginning. I will now wait patiently on Thee. I will trust Thee. I know You will come help me. Come, Lord.

■ TRUTHS TO LIVE BY

Troubles teach us trust. As God shows His presence in our toughest moments, we identify Him as our personal deliverer and source of help. Trusting Him becomes a habit of life. Moments of trouble force us to review past experiences and learn the lesson of trust anew, but God's work in our terrible moments teaches us to trust.

Troubles feed our testimony. Testimony for God must be more than talking from a book, even from the Bible. Testimony must say what God has done for me personally. God's actions in my troubles give content as I share with others how great God is.

Trouble is never too tough for God. God proves Himself to be our God as He does God-sized work to deliver us. We do not trust God if we expect Him to do only what we or another person could do. Trust in God expects God to do work only He can do. God proves up to the task. He delivers in the most horrible times.

■ A VERSE TO REMEMBER

Blessed is that man that maketh the LORD *his trust, and respecteth not the proud, nor such as turn aside to lies.*
—Psalm 40:4

■ DAILY BIBLE READINGS

Obey God's Laws

PSALM 119:1-16,45,105,129-130

The Bible. Good vibrations tremble their way from our head down our spine to our toes. Bible is one of those good words. Like apple pie and motherhood, you are just naturally pro-Bible. God wants more. God wants testimony of what the Bible has done in your life. When did Bible reading show you where God was at work, a promise God had for you, a decision you needed to make, a hope you could cling to, and forgiveness that freed you from guilt? The longest chapter in the Bible is personal testimony to what God's Word did in one person's life. Is it time to sit down and write your own testimony about the Bible's power in your experience with God?

■ THE BIBLE LESSON

1 Blessed are the undefiled in the way, who walk in the law of the Lord.

2 Blessed are they that keep his testimonies, and that seek him with the whole heart.

3 They also do no iniquity: they walk in his ways.

4 Thou hast commanded us to keep thy precepts diligently.

5 O that my ways were directed to keep thy statutes!

6 Then shall I not be ashamed, when I have respect unto all thy commandments.

7 I will praise thee with uprightness of heart, when I shall have learned thy righteous judgments.

8 I will keep thy statutes: O forsake me not utterly.

9 Wherewithal shall a young man cleanse his way? by taking heed thereto according to thy word.

10 With my whole heart have I sought thee: O let me not wander from thy commandments.

11 Thy word have I hid in mine heart, that I might not sin against thee.

12 Blessed art thou, O Lord: teach me thy statutes.

13 With my lips have I declared all the judgments of thy mouth.

14 I have rejoiced in the way of thy testimonies, as much as in all riches.

15 I will meditate in thy precepts, and have respect unto thy ways.
16 I will delight myself in thy statutes: I will not forget thy word.

. . . .

45 And I will walk at liberty: for I seek thy precepts.

. . . . , ...

105 Thy word is a lamp unto my feet, and a light unto my path.

. . . .

129 Thy testimonies are wonderful: therefore doth my soul keep them.
130 The entrance of thy words giveth light; it giveth understanding
unto the simple.

■ THE LESSON EXPLAINED

Bible Brings Blessing (vv. 1–8)

The Bible points the way to the happy life experiencing God's
power and direction each day. Such a life has several marks. It
obeys God's teachings. It seeks to know God personally and live out
the lifestyle the Bible describes. It refuses to let sin characterize life.
It prays for help in obeying God's Word. It walks confidently without
shame before a world opposed to God's Word. It gives praise to God
and calls on Him to be present, not forsaking me in time of trouble.

Bible Cleanses My Ways (vv. 9–16)

I have human ways. I sin and depart from God's Word.
Reading the Word shows me God's ways, forgiving ways, cleansing ways. In them I find anew the path back to God for forgiveness, cleansing, and renewal. Such cleansing comes only when I
wholeheartedly commit myself to God and His Word. How can I
do that? By memorizing the Word, so that it is fresh in my heart
any time sin tempts me. By asking God to teach me not only the
words of the Bible but the meaning of those words for my life.
By sharing the Word with others, for as I share the Word I learn
more about it and let it become central to who I am and what I
do. By rejoicing in God's Word and letting it bring me happiness, realizing that the happiness the world and its riches
promise will never come true. By studying and meditating on
God's Word so that I understand it more deeply and find it
working in my life more often. By remembering God's Word so

it is effective in my life and not just something I claim to believe when others ask.

Bible Eases Away Enemies (vv. 41–48)

I face opposition. Everyone does not love me all the time. Especially when I follow God's Word, others follow me with ridicule, hatred, and reproach. What do I do? I read God's Word anew and find fresh assurance that God is love, that He is loyal to His covenant, and that He wants a love relationship with me. He wants salvation to be real each day of my life. Such salvation delivers me from everything enemies plan for me. I depend on God's Word being available in time of trouble. It shows me how God judges or rules in each situation and gives me confidence as I apply His Word to tough decisions in the face of opposition. How can I expect this wonderful Word of God to do this for me? By committing myself to be true to it always. Then what happens? I know true liberty or freedom. I do not have to walk in tight, restricted places. I have the breadth and depth of God's loving will to walk in as I set my course according to His Word. Such freedom gives courage to testify before whomever I meet, even royalty. How can I do that? Because I love God's Word, a love that comes not from someone else teaching me I should love it, but from my own personal experience with God's Word. Reading God's Word and living God's Word result in loving God's Word.

Bible Lights up Life (vv. 105, 129–130)

Wonderful. That's the only word that describes the Word, for the Bible makes me full of wonder at how great God is. God gives me the Bible. The Bible sheds God-sized light beams ahead of me, showing the way through life and making it bright. No wonder my heart longs for and pants after God's Word. I want to know it better than anything else. I want to be an expert in God's Word, not only in knowledge but most of all in application. I want the Word to reveal anew God's mercy and lighten my path so I obey God and do not sin. I sob and weep because I am not able to obey perfectly. Teach me Thy Word, God. Only as You teach me can I obey and not sin. Light up my life!

■ TRUTHS TO LIVE BY

The Bible is to be read and obeyed, not adored. Too often we speak more about the Bible than we let the Bible speak to our lives. God gave us His wonderful Word to change our lives and keep us in love relationship with Him.

The Bible makes salvation real. Reading the Bible lets God talk to me personally and show me what He is doing in my life and in my world to change me and redeem His world. I do not feel the dynamic reality of salvation if I do not hear God's voice each day.

The Bible keeps me from sinning. I try to depend on my own power not to sin. I think I am strong enough to obey. Experience proves me wrong. Only as I gain new direction and encouragement from God through His Word each day can I be the person God wants me to be, obeying Him and experiencing Him.

■ A VERSE TO REMEMBER

Thy word is a lamp unto my feet, and a light unto my path.—
Psalm 119:105

■ DAILY BIBLE READINGS

Aug. 5 — Keep God's Laws. Deut. 26:15–19
Aug. 6 — Be Strong and of Good Courage. Josh. 1:1–9
Aug. 7 — Better Than Sacrifice. 1 Sam. 15:22–29
Aug. 8 — Ready for Rain. Gen. 6:11–22
Aug. 9 — Nothing Left Undone. Josh. 11:10–15
Aug. 10 — Holding Fast to the Lord. 2 Kings 18:1–8
Aug. 11 — Learned Obedience. Heb. 5:1–10

Repent and Confess
PSALM 51

God teaches lessons in strange ways. He sent me to New Mexico to meet Henry Blackaby and learn how to write notes for *The Experiencing God Study Bible*. At least that is how it appeared to me. I was ready for the most exciting challenge of my life. I got all my notes, listened to Henry every chance I got, and had a good time reliving past New Mexico memories with my wife. Then God revealed why I was in New Mexico. I needed to experience Him.

For too many months I had been coasting on my religious laurels. I knew enough religion to get by and fool people at work and at church, even to fool myself for a while. Then God spoke to me through Henry. When have I seen God at work? When have I really been in love with Him, experiencing the love relationship He is working to establish? When have I heard Him invite me to join Him where He is at work? When has He spoken directly to me and revealed Himself, His ways, and His purposes to me? When has God been real enough in my life that an invitation from Him has forced a crisis of belief requiring faith and action from me? When have I shown enough faith to make life adjustments God required of me to join in His work? When have I really experienced the reality of God through obeying Him and seeing Him work through my life?

I had to drop to my knees and confess my sins of ignoring God and trying to coast to heaven on past experiences. I had to ask Him to let me truly experience Him. I had to repent.

■ THE BIBLE LESSON

To the chief Musician, A Psalm of David, when Nathan the prophet came unto him, after he had gone in to Bath–sheba

1 *Have mercy upon me, O God, according to thy loving-kindness: according unto the multitude of thy tender mercies blot out my transgressions.*

2 Wash me thoroughly from mine iniquity, and cleanse me from my sin.

3 For I acknowledge my transgressions: and my sin is ever before me.

4 Against thee, thee only, have I sinned, and done this evil in thy sight: that thou mightest be justified when thou speakest, and be clear when thou judgest.

5 Behold, I was shapen in iniquity; and in sin did my mother conceive me.

6 Behold, thou desirest truth in the inward parts: and in the hidden part thou shalt make me to know wisdom.

7 Purge me with hyssop, and I shall be clean: wash me, and I shall be whiter than snow.

8 Make me to hear joy and gladness; that the bones which thou hast broken may rejoice.

9 Hide thy face from my sins, and blot out all mine iniquities.

10 Create in me a clean heart, O God; and renew a right spirit within me.

11 Cast me not away from thy presence; and take not thy holy spirit from me.

12 Restore unto me the joy of thy salvation; and uphold me with thy free spirit.

13 Then will I teach transgressors thy ways; and sinners shall be converted unto thee.

. . . .

17 The sacrifices of God are a broken spirit: a broken and a contrite heart, O God, thou wilt not despise.

■ THE LESSON EXPLAINED

Repentance Describes Personal Sin (vv. 1–5)

Sin is real. It ruins my life. It separates me from God. Even when I talk a lot about God, I am still not close to Him because I have sin I refuse to admit. God, have mercy. Show Your love to me again. Scrub my sin away until I am as perfectly clean as You want me to be. Sin has become the dominating reality of my life. Only You can get rid of it because sin is between You and me. I refused to do and be what You expected in our love relationship. I may have done something bad to other people, but the basic fact is that I did it because I was disobeying you. As long as I can remember, clear back to my mother's womb, I have gone my way and not yours. Forgive me. Cleanse me. Now.

Repentance Opens the Door to Joy and Purity (vv. 6–12)

I know what You want, God. You want me devoted to Your truth through and through. You want to be able to trust me totally, always. I cannot be that by myself. You have to wash me and start over anew with me. Do so, God. Only then can I experience true joy and gladness for they come from You, from a love experience with You, from obeying You. Get my sins where You will never see them again. Yes, You who know all, I want You to forget all my sins forever. Make me clean. Make me think, act, plan, and be what You and Your Spirit want me to be. Let Your Spirit direct my life. Don't take Your Spirit away from me, ever. Make me to be what You want me to be.

Repentance Raises You to Report (vv. 13–19)

Repentance is not just a private thing between You and me, Lord. It changes me. Everybody will see something different in me. I will tell them everything You have done for me. I will lead other sinners to the love relationship You have shared with me. You want more from me than going to church and doing what people do there. You want me to tell others about You and Your love. I will, Lord, starting right now.

Why? My heart is broken. You are repairing it and making it what You want. When I turn back to You, admit my sins, and depend on You for forgiveness and renewal, I know You will restore the relationship between us. You will accept my worship and move mightily among the people I know. Forgive me. Renew me. Direct me. I sinned. Don't let me do it again.

■ TRUTHS TO LIVE BY

God, in love, waits for sinners. You need no appointment. Any time is the right time to tell God about your sins and repent. He will forgive you now.

God is deeply involved with your sin. Sin is not something between you and another person. Sin is always primarily a matter with you and God. Repent and straighten things out with Him. Then He will send you to straighten things out with the people involved.

God has great plans for a repentant you. God does not want you to remain in your sin. He wants you to know the joy of experiencing Him in obedience. Only your sin separates you from joy. Repent now.

■ A VERSE TO REMEMBER

Create in me a clean heart, O God: and renew a right spirit within me.—Psalm 51:10

■ DAILY BIBLE READINGS

Aug. 12 — Repentance the Only Hope. Ezek. 18:25–32
Aug. 13 — Rend Hearts, Not Garments. Joel 2:10–14
Aug. 14 — No Exemptions. Luke 13:1–5
Aug. 15 — All May Be Saved. Rom. 10:5–13
Aug. 16 — Sin Acknowledged. Ps. 32:1–5
Aug. 17 — Renewal of Israel. Ezek. 36:22–28
Aug. 18 — Transgressions Swept Away. Isa. 44:18–23

Worship and Witness
PSALM 96

God is so good. Each moment spent with Him fills me with elation. He does not have to do something spectacular. Just being with Him makes me want to share with the world the wonder of Him and of His love. Feeling His power as I let Him lead me to write these lessons makes me shout out loud about how great my God is. Come, get to know Him. Come, find a love relationship with Him. Tell everybody about Him. Knowing Him is the most exciting experience in the world. I hope you feel that same excitement because you know Him, too.

■ THE BIBLE LESSON

1 O sing unto the Lord a new song: sing unto the Lord, all the earth.

2 Sing unto the Lord, bless his name; show forth his salvation from day to day.

3 Declare his glory among the heathen, his wonders among all people.

4 For the Lord is great, and greatly to be praised: he is to be feared above all gods.

5 For all the gods of the nations are idols: but the Lord made the heavens.

6 Honor and majesty are before him: strength and beauty are in his sanctuary.

7 Give unto the Lord, O ye kindreds of the people, give unto the Lord glory and strength.

8 Give unto the Lord the glory due unto his name: bring an offering, and come into his courts.

9 O worship the Lord in the beauty of holiness: fear before him, all the earth.

10 Say among the heathen that the Lord reigneth: the world also shall be established that it shall not be moved: he shall judge the people righteously.

11 Let the heavens rejoice, and let the earth be glad; let the sea roar, and the fullness thereof.

12 *Let the field be joyful, and all that is therein: then shall all the trees of the wood rejoice*

13 *Before the Lord: for he cometh, for he cometh to judge the earth: he shall judge the world with righteousness, and the people with his truth.*

■ THE LESSON EXPLAINED

Worship Causes Me to Witness (vv. 1–3)

Get out of your old rut with God. He is about to do something new for you. You do something new for Him. Shout, sing, tell everyone about how good God is. Every day of your life, show other people what God has done to bring salvation to you. If you have been in God's presence, you have fallen down before Him in worship, exclaiming about how wonderful He is. That sense of wonder and awe should fill your life as you go back out into the world where people do not know Jesus. Oh, God, I want everyone who has never heard about you to know the story of Jesus. I want them to experience your salvation. Help me tell them.

Worship Belongs to God Alone (vv. 4–6)

You know I tell a lot of stories, God, but none as exciting as the story of Your salvation. No one in heaven or on earth approaches You. Lots of people and things try to take Your place. Money, social status, family, job, politicians, sports, clothes, jewelry, personal appearance, ego—so many candidates to be god in my life. None measure up. None have Your love, Your power, Your control over all the universe. You created everything. No one else did. How could I possibly have any other god? I come to Your house to worship. Your beauty surrounds me. Your glory, that weighty presence that gives you a presence and power beyond anyone else, overwhelms me. Worship makes me know again. No one is like You. You are unique. What can I do to let everyone know?

Worship Is Public, Not Private (vv. 7–9)

God, I would not dare be selfish and keep all this to myself. I want everyone to join in. I will shout out to the whole world, all the families of nations, that You are present in Your worship place. Let all come and sing about Your greatness. You alone deserve the highest reputation as holy, glorious, powerful Ruler of the universe. Let's invite everybody to come before You in fear, in reverence, in awe, in wonder, yes, in worship. Of course, when we come, we will bring the best things You have given us and give them back to You. We could never worship without symbolically showing how much You mean by giving You the best we have. For You have given it all to us. What a glorious sight, all the world falling down in worship before You.

Worship Prepares for the Judge to Come (vv. 10–13)

God, so many people do not know You. Nations, whole people groups, have never heard about You. We must tell them before it is too late. They must know that You and You alone rule this world, that You are responsible for the trust we can place in the world. You put it in place. You keep it in place.

But You will do more. You will show Your demands for justice and righteousness. You will come to bring a close to the sinfulness of this world. Yes, You are coming. Let the world and every component in it rejoice. You will establish the world the way You want it, the way we want it, too. You will give us a world of peace and justice. Your truth and faithfulness will control everything that exists. O God, You are so marvelous. Let's sing Your praises. Let's tell everybody. God is coming to judge the world. Praise Him.

■ TRUTHS TO LIVE BY

God's presence leads to worship. When you know God personally, when you stand in His presence, you react naturally. You sing His glory and shout aloud at His goodness. You can do nothing else.

God's presence leads to witness. When you worship, you witness. You can do nothing else. God makes such a marvelous impression on your life, you have to tell someone. Silence is not an option.

God's presence points to His coming. This world is not what you want it to be and certainly not what God wants it to be. He will change that. He is coming in judgment to create anew His world. Are you ready?

■ A VERSE TO REMEMBER

Sing unto the LORD, bless his name; shew forth his salvation from day to day.—Psalm 96:2.

■ DAILY BIBLE READINGS

Aug. 19 — In Spirit, the Only Way. John 4:19–26
Aug. 20 — A Warm Invitation. Ps. 95:1–7
Aug. 21 — Preparation Required. Ps. 96:1–9
Aug. 22 — Heaven's Command. Rev. 14:1–7
Aug. 23 — All People to Be Told. Isa. 43:8–13
Aug. 24 — Appointed to Witness. Acts 22:6–16
Aug. 25 — Make Disciples to All Nations. Matt. 28:16–20

Sexual Purity

**MATTHEW 19:4-6;
1 CORINTHIANS 6:13B,18-20;
ROMANS 12:1-2**

What is the greatest gift a person ever gave me? How would you answer? Four responses fly to my mind: •My mother's suffering and patient waiting to give me life. •My wife's continual giving of herself to me. •My wife's gift of two handsome, healthy sons.

Suddenly I realize the answers all have something in common: Human life is the most precious gift. Ultimately, we know life is God's gift to us humans. That one sentence floods us with responsibility and meaning. How precious is life? What is more valuable than life: money, time, escape from pain, escape from responsibility, career? Do I want anything so much I am willing to sacrifice a life to control it or achieve it?

Again, when I have the gift of life, how do I treat this most precious gift I have received? With greater care than anything else I have? The Bible shows us answers to these kinds of questions in many ways. The passages we study this week point us to one way of treating the gift of life God has given, the area of sexual purity.

■ THE BIBLE LESSON

4 And he answered and said unto them, Have ye not read, that he which made them at the beginning made them male and female,

5 And said, For this cause shall a man leave father and mother, and shall cleave to his wife: and they twain shall be one flesh?

6 Wherefore they are no more twain, but one flesh. What therefore God hath joined together, let not man put asunder.

. . . .

13b Now the body is not for fornication, but for the Lord; and the Lord for the body.

. . . .

18 Flee fornication. Every sin that a man doeth is without the body;

but he that committeth fornication sinneth against his own body.

19 *What? know ye not that your body is the temple of the Holy Ghost which is in you, which ye have of God, and ye are not your own?*

20 *For ye are bought with a price: therefore glorify God in your body, and in your spirit, which are God's.*

. . . . , ...

1 *I beseech you therefore, brethren, by the mercies of God, that ye present your bodies a living sacrifice, holy, acceptable unto God, which is your reasonable service.*

2 *And be not conformed to this world: but be ye transformed by the renewing of your mind, that ye may prove what is that good, and acceptable, and perfect, will of God.*

■ THE LESSON EXPLAINED
Pure Forever (Matt. 19:4–6)

Jesus has to be wrong about something, they said. Surely we can find some weakness we can exploit. So the Pharisees, the Jewish religious experts, repeatedly came to Jesus with questions. They did not want answers; they wanted victory in a game of words and rules. The Pharisees themselves had no sure answer to the question. They turned to Deuteronomy 24:1 and then interpreted it in two ways. One said a wife could be divorced only for sexual impurity. The other said a wife could be divorced for almost any reason, even serving bad food. Jesus said that to understand the Bible you must look at the larger picture in the Bible, not just one verse. Where did marriage start? At creation, of course. How did God paint marriage? As two people so committed that one left the deepest relationship in life, that with parents, to achieve an even deeper relationship, that with spouse. The two should join together in sexual relations and in all other relationships to form the closest unity human beings can form with one another.

God alone can achieve such close union. It is His gift. How dare any individual try to break up what God has created! How dare any person try to have sexual union without the life-long commitment to be one flesh forever! Sexual relationship is God's way of cementing the relationship together at its deepest level.

Pure for the Lord (1 Cor. 6:13b,18–20)

How can you be sure you will not be part of God's kingdom? Paul bluntly described several ways (vv. 9–10). Fornication, or sinning by having sexual relationships of any kind outside marriage, heads the list. Why? Because a Christian believer has dedicated the body to God. The body is prepared for God's use and eventually for God to resurrect it to eternal life (see v. 14). The body is joined with Christ as part of His bride the church. The body is where Christ's promised Holy Spirit lives to direct your life. Your body is not a possession you own to do with it as you like. Your body is a gift from God. He owns it. He bought it for Himself on the cross of Calvary.

The body has one use and one function: to glorify God. Sexual union with a spouse fulfills that function, for that is what God intended. Any other kind of sexual activity shames God, for it violates God's purpose and plan for you, going against what God knows is best for you. Sexual purity is a necessity, for sexual relationships involve the body God bought, God wants to use for His glory, and God will resurrect to eternity. If God is so interested in your body, how could you possibly use your body in shameful acts He condemns?

Pure for Worship (Rom. 12:1–2)

God wants one thing from you: an attitude of sacrificial service. Romans sings the song of justification by faith for eleven chapters and then begs you to do what is clearly reasonable: submit your bodies, yourselves, as sacrifices on God's altar. Only in this way can you worship (the basic meaning of "service") God in a manner that is sane and reasonable. To use your body in an impure manner in sexual acts outside marriage and then come to worship God is insane. It is the world's way of acting and debating.

Can you do something other than the way all the world does it? Certainly. God in Christ has transformed you, totally changed you. That is the work of His Spirit within you. He changes your will. With your body you live out a life of purity, proving to the world by personal example what God's perfect will for people is.

■ TRUTHS TO LIVE BY

Sexual purity is God's only way without exception. God gave you the supreme gift of life. He also gives you the supreme relationship of sexual union in marriage, the ultimate sign of total commitment to one person. Outside a lifelong commitment to a spouse, sexual acts cannot symbolize the eternal union God has created.

Sexual purity is demanded if God is to live in you. The holy God cannot abide sin. He chooses to make your body His dwelling place on earth. Dare you dirty up the place where God wants to live? Could you ever say that the Spirit of God told me to enter a sexual relationship outside marriage?

Sexual purity shows your dedication to worship God. God wants everything you do to demonstrate worship for Him. Sexual acts outside marriage can in no way be claimed as acts of worship. That is the worst kind of pagan religion.

■ A VERSE TO REMEMBER

For ye are bought with a price: therefore glorify God in Your body, and in your spirit, which are God's.
—1 Corinthians 6:20

■ DAILY BIBLE READINGS

Jan. 15 — God's Historical Faithfulness. Isa. 49:7–13
Jan. 16 — God Does Not Forget. Isa. 49:14–18
Jan. 17 — God's Restoration. Isa. 49:19–26
Jan. 18 — God Reaches Out to All People. Isa. 56:1–8
Jan. 19 — God Against Idolatry. Isa. 57:1–13
Jan. 20 — God Ready to Heal. Isa. 57:14–21
Jan. 21 — Kindness Is Better Than Fasting. Isa. 58:1–14